BOOKS BY

ROBERT T. PETERSSON

The Art of Ecstasy: Teresa, Bernini, and Crashaw   1970

Sir Kenelm Digby: The Ornament of England   1956

EDITOR

Shakespeare, KING RICHARD II (*Yale Shakespeare Series*)   1957

The Art of Ecstasy
Teresa, Bernini, and Crashaw

The Art of Ecstasy
Teresa, Bernini, and Crashaw

ROBERT T. PETERSSON

ATHENEUM   NEW YORK

1974

TO SUZY

It is amazing how compact a unity every historical epoch presents throughout its various manifestations. One and the same inspiration, one and the same biological style, are recognizable in several branches of art.

Ortega y Gasset

. . . one art mixing with the other and all together producing a state different from one of aesthetic comprehension.

Roger Fry

Preface

This is one of the first extended attempts to relate works of art from different media. The primary material is the autobiography of St Teresa of Ávila and (deriving from it) Bernini's Cornaro Chapel in Rome and Richard Crashaw's English poetry. Written originally as the opening essay of a connected series, the study gradually outgrew itself and now becomes part of a larger plan to examine several late-Renaissance works in various artistic modes.

What attracted me initially was Teresa herself – the woman in her writing and in her unusual religious experience. At about the same time, I also become aware of her presence in two remarkable productions by a sculptor-architect and a poet. Seventy years after she died and thirty years after she was sainted, these works by Bernini and Crashaw appeared. Far from being skilful imitations of her experience or pious gestures toward it, they are re-creations of the experience into works totally and intensely their own. It is as though each man became the experience he expressed. (At one point I considered calling the book *Ecstasy into Art*, on the model of Sir Kenneth Clark's on landscape.) Here was the occasion to explore not only the very congenial material of Teresa's *Vida* but also the rare cultural phenomenon of two nearly simultaneous renderings of a subject in different art media and in entirely independent circumstances. The presentation raised serious problems, however.

First one must be clear about what a comparison is and how it works. Basically it is the relationship between unlike things which also possess essential likeness, and it works as a means of exploring the nature of both things, or of opening up one thing by means of another. To see this is to appreciate the value of restraint in comparison, for clearly the objective is exploration and not the demonstration of ultimate likeness.

Then, however, if the reader expects a systematic theory of how works in different art media should be related, he will be disappointed. Although most of the dangers and delusions involved have been made reasonably clear, especially by René Wellek and Rensselaer Lee, no theory of procedures has yet emerged. As Wellek says, 'there is no particular theoretical problem in the fact that the arts are in constant interrelationship, as are all human activities.' But many difficulties raised by the *paragone* literature of the Renaissance and seventeenth century still exist today. Nor, for good reasons, is the prospect of arriving at a comprehensive, workable theory very bright and immediate. Basic differences in the various art forms of various eras (which also reflect divergent attitudes toward art in different eras) make the problem complicated enough, but also we have no settled purposes for making the comparisons. By now, many attempts have been made to find the basis for procedure. Form, style, purpose, subject matter, and the concept of time, have all been used as indexes for comparison, and so have analogies to life patterns and commonness of moral or spiritual attitude. Thus far, the best basis has proved to be subject matter. Conceivably the most fruitful comparison would involve more than subject matter. Rensselaer Lee's formulation (and I know no better starting point) includes subject matter, a common purpose, and the 'great middle-ground of human content,' by which he seems to mean those motives, emotions, and actions which can be shared by, let us say, a poem and a painting.

Also we now recognize the diverse ways in which art is perceived, if we allow, with E. H. Gombrich, that the work of art is fulfilled by the beholder – by the individual perceiver. Until the grounds of comparison become clearer than at present, we are thrown back on our resources of invention, taste, and judgment. If theory is to advance, our means for advancing it is through the experience of specific instances. Here I have proceeded on the best assumptions I could build up around the special situation. Though parallel situations have assisted me, in this study the method is essentially empirical.

There are those who have an aversion to the very idea of comparing works of art taken from different modes. They have a point. Comparison is an uncertain and vexatious operation. It pulls things out of shape, and the lack of criteria invites the critic to pick up a thesis and run away with it. A poem is, after all, not a painting, and a poem which is too like a painting can never achieve great excellence. Pattern poems, musical tone poems, painting of sound, loquacious operas, plot-heavy ballets – these, by neglecting the qualities belonging to one art, are usually mediocre. Suzanne Langer is probably right, that no combination of media can succeed unless one predominates. Even opera, traditionally the optimal expression of combined media, shows the need of a single predominance, for no *Gesamtkunstwerk*, merely by combining different arts, ever approached the universality Johann Mattheson intended for it. The temporal arts of poetry and music, and the spatial arts of painting and sculpture, differ in fundamental ways. There need be no quarrel with this position – except that it is incomplete, and not entirely lifelike. One persuasive reason 'the arts are in constant interrelationship' is that our senses naturally interrelate and interfuse. St Anselm argued in the twelfth century that things which stimulate many senses are more harmful than those which stimulate one. It is dangerous, he thought, to sit in a garden smelling and seeing roses, hearing songs and stories. However prudent his advice may be, it has met with little favour through the centuries.

In a wider view, some artists believe that there exists an invisible centre from which all arts arise. Like Baudelaire, Wallace Stevens talks about 'an unascertained and fundamental aesthetic, or order, of which poetry and painting are manifestations, but of which, for that matter, sculpture or music or any other aesthetic realization would equally be a manifestation.' We need not accept this or any other holistic view of art to be convinced that, to a greater or lesser degree, art media have affected each other ever since antiquity. We think of Simonides in the sixth century B.C. as the first to state that 'painting is mute poetry, poetry a speaking picture.' Signs of close association have been evident from the beginning, in epics sung to accompaniment, in the elaborate spectacle of a Greek tragedy. (It is interesting, and partially relevant, that γράφειν meant both to write and to paint, and I am told that the single Chinese verb *hsieh* also has both meanings.) In more recent centuries one need only think of Michelangelo, Shakespeare, Rubens, Bernini, Milton, Bach, Wagner, Gide, and Picasso to establish that the work of major artists in one medium has been strongly affected by another. One need only look at a few good late-Renaissance churches to see how successfully architecture, painting, and sculpture may become a unity. In the baroque era what can we possibly call the Baldacchino or the Cathedra Petri in St Peter's? Are they architecture, or sculpture, or both of these and more? In fact we have no words to describe them. Once we acknowledge that different senses and different art forms can combine and influence each other, it follows that comparisons will be made. The wonder is that anyone should object on principle to the act of comparing works from different media. It may be that careless and fanciful efforts have blinded us to what is possible. And sometimes it seems as if a too protective regard for the special field has fostered a professional resistance to the idea. Even comparative literature may be ruled out.

The works presently before us all belong to the sixteenth and seventeenth centuries – the era of Renaissance and Baroque which Panofsky, in contrast to Wölfflin, regarded as a single movement with two great climaxes. As Rensselaer Lee makes conspicuously clear, the doctrine of *ut pictura poesis*, which conceived of art as the ideal imitation of human life, dominated the era. The effect of this humanistic theory of art, revived from Aristotle and Horace, was to make the connections between arts especially close during that two-century span of time, for the theory prevailed not only in painting but in other arts as well. There poured forth an abundance of fused forms of art, of synaesthesia, of works which take for granted that one art participates in the nature of another, and in these we sometimes see expressed the belief that man is a unified being, a unity of body and soul, of the many senses, and of the senses and mind. In many countries emblem books appeared: poems with matching illustrations. French dirges were written as dances *en forme d'allemande*, and French poems were often called *tableaux* or *portraits*. Montaigne spoke of writing as painting, and many authors after him referred to their writing as painting, sculpture, and architecture, among them, Marino, Quevedo, Du Perron, Hofmannswaldau, Jerónimo Baía, and Jean Auvray. In a sonnet, Lope de Vega describes Marino as 'a great painter for the ears' and Rubens as 'a great poet for the eyes', and Marino himself, who divided the poems of his *Galleria* into 'Pitture' and 'Sculture,' asks a painter to help him depict the death of Adonis, and in the process makes a pun on *penna* (pen) and *pennello* (brush). Marino influenced not only English, French, and German poets, but Poussin and other painters; yet it is one thing for

Poussin to call himself a 'painter of the passions,' and another for the dramatist Racine to do so. Marino understood poetry to imitate qualities of the body and painting qualities of the soul: *l'una fa quasi intendere co' sensi, l'altra sentire cõ intelletto* – 'one causes us almost to understand with our senses, the other to feel with our intellect.' And however the theory holds, the words sound strikingly like Eliot on Metaphysical poetry, or Pound on Remy de Gourmont.

The Teresan works of Bernini and Crashaw offer us an almost perfect case for comparison.* Since no direct links exist between either the artists or their works, the two exhibit resemblances which transcend differences of individual temperament, nationality, and artistic medium. What the comparison is able to achieve cannot be easily stated. Of that my whole book is a statement. It may be that the most valuable result is a fuller realization of the works as such. At least I have conscientiously tried not to press any baroque thesis but to let the works speak for themselves. Second, it tells us something about both literal and metaphorical or symbolic likenesses (here I lump together the latter two). Though the phrase may sound provocative, I am persuaded that in many minds there is more confusion than necessary about the difference between metaphorical or symbolic likenesses which are merely imaginary, and those which genuinely exist in works. If not quite every work of art, then certainly every religious work of art, is necessarily symbolic in some respects. It is 'unitive vision' which defines the total reality of Teresa, Bernini, and Crashaw, and gives to their art its strongly metaphorical and transcendental qualities. (The comparison seems to show, by the way, that there is no difficulty in transferring some of Wölfflin's principles from art to literature.)

Finally the comparison tells us something about a seventeenth-century *Zeitgeist*, if one should grant that such exists. Whatever we think about it, an age is something actual, and something actual has a nature, inscrutable as it may be. To deny existence to the *Zeitgeist* is scarcely more useful than denying existence to such concepts as *soul*, because we cannot define it well. Professor Gombrich's recent Deneke Lecture indicates, though

* As far as I know, the comparison was first pointed out by Mario Praz in *Secentismo e Marinismo in Inghilterra* (Florence, 1925), pp. 145ff. Since then Austin Warren, Jean Hagstrum, Howard Hibbard, and others have made reference to it.

perhaps with an excessive amount of anti-Hegelianism, that generalizations about the *Zeitgeist* demand of us a steady and strenuous scepticism. No matter how far we progress, where the spirit of an age is concerned we should accustom ourselves to inconclusiveness. What F. L. Lucas said about Hume and others applies here: 'life can be lived with far fewer certainties than is commonly supposed'! My own opinion accords with Ernst Kitzinger's: 'A *Zeitgeist* may be an historian's construct – a mere methodological crutch – but I do not see how any really deep and meaningful interpretation of a major historical style can do without it or some equivalent term.'

It may be superfluous to observe that 'Baroque' too is a useful word which is probably not definable. Although I am at pains to indicate some of its leading features, it has not been my intention to define it.

* * *

In the course of work I have been generously supported by the Guggenheim Foundation (1958-1959) and by Smith College, with both sabbatical leaves and funds granted by the Committee on Aid to Faculty Research. I thank them, and I also thank the proficient and devoted librarians who have helped me, at the Frick Art Reference Library in New York, the Warburg Institute Library (and Photographic Collection) in London, the American Academy in Rome, and the Smith College Library in Northampton, Massachusetts.

Scholars in various fields have also given me invaluable criticism. The manuscript has been read, completely or in part, by Martin Price (Department of English, Yale University), Juan Avalle-Arce (Department of Romance Languages, University of North Carolina, recently of Smith College), Sister Teresa Waldman (Nazareth College, Kalamazoo, Michigan), Jochanan H. A. Wijnhoven (Department of Religion, Smith College), Frank Kermode (University College, London University), Mrs Harry Craig (presently in Rome), and Irving Lavin (Institute of Fine Arts, New York University). Professor Lavin, whose forthcoming book on Bernini's Cornaro Chapel will be definitive, has given me unusually full and helpful advice on Bernini and related subjects, and with openhanded generosity. In addition I wish to acknowledge those authors, besides René Wellek and Rensselaer Lee, whose work has assisted me most: Father Trueman Dicken, E. H. Gombrich, Allison Peers, Herbert Read, Austin Warren, and Rudolf Wittkower. Professor Wittkower's writing on Bernini and *seicento* Italy is so knowing and perceptive as to have made an entirely new beginning impossible.

For their unusual care and intelligence, and for their belief in books, I also thank Mr Colin Franklin, Mr Harry Ford, and other editors of Routledge and of Atheneum. Last, I wish to thank Suzy, for her endless help, and for her deep humanistic sense of art, scholarship, and the writer's deficiencies. The dish would be poorer had she not constantly stirred and seasoned it.

R.T.P.

Rome

Contents

Plates

Acknowledgements

I acknowledge with thanks the following sources of photographs: for the colour transparency (printed as the Frontispiece) Mr. Ernest Nash and the Fototeca Unione (Rome), and for the monochrome prints:

Gabinetto Fotografico Nazionale (Rome): 52482, 55221, 52498, 52495, 52520, 52516, 52503, 52513, 52515, 52497, 52529, 52486, 52487, 52490, 55227, appearing as Plates II, III, V, IX, X, XI, XII, XIV, XV, XVIII, XX, XXII, XXIV, XXV, and XXVI.

Alinari, now including Anderson (Florence): Anderson 197 and 2391, appearing as Plates VIII and XIII; Alinari 5922, 5911, 28313, 28316, 6193b, appearing as Plates VI, VII, XVI, XVII, and XXIII.

Fototeca Unione (Rome): 10101 FG appears as Plate IV.

Giordano Falzoni (Rome): print for Plate XXI and XXVII.

Life Magazine (Dmitri Kessel, 20 April 1962): print for Plate XIX.

Martin Hürlimann, *España; Paisajes, Monumentos, Tradiciones* (2nd ed. Barcelona, 1958): print for Plate I.

E. W. Trueman Dicken, *The Crucible of Love* (London and New York, 1963): print for Plate XXVIII.

Part I

The New Carmelite

1 A View of Ávila, north wall of the city

One

Teresa's Spain

The map of Spain rises to the *meseta central*, the high and vast tableland overlooking the rest of the Iberian peninsula. This inland half of the country, split roughly into Old and New Castile by ragged sierras, is cut off by mountains on all sides but the west where the land falls off gradually towards the Atlantic. From here the Castilian language and spirit have dominated the entire Spanish world. Much of the territory was traversed for more than fifteen years by St Teresa of Ávila. Her long work of reform was carried out despite the obstacles of poverty, illness, hardship, and the interference of both ecclesiastical and civil authorities. She crossed and recrossed it through dust, floods, snow, and burning heat. Seen partly in El Greco, partly in backgrounds of Velázquez portraits, that country has long been known as 'the land of saints and stones' – *la tierra de santos y de cantos*. Teresa was a saint of extraordinary obstinacy and efficiency, a mystic of phenomenal lucidity and intensity, a woman whose energy, humour, and common sense were legendary even while she lived. She was the outstanding provincial genius of the Counter-Reformation.[1]

Supported at first by only a few clerical and lay friends, beginning only with four orphan girls she took as novices, Teresa founded thirty-two convents and monasteries. Along the way she managed conventual affairs, laboured hard with her hands, instructed and encouraged those around her, and not least, wrote prolifically. By the time she died in 1582 she had successfully reformed the entire Carmelite order.[2]

The tannish grey fortress-city of Ávila built on the hard ground of Castile was the centre of all her activities (PLATE I). Though born in a small town of the province, Teresa was brought up in Ávila, in a large Christian family of partly Jewish origin – wealthy from commerce and

3

tithe-farming, but neither noble nor aristocratic, as was formerly believed. The expulsion of the Jews notwithstanding, many a Spanish family had Jewish blood, not least the families of Vives, Fernando de Rojas, Luis de León, and Montaigne, whose mother was the daughter of a Spanish exile.[3] It is clear that Teresa's writing was affected by her being 'another great figure in the Christian-Oriental line.'[4] Her mysticism is coloured by Islamic and Judaic influences. The grand theme of Christian life culminating in the *unión mística* is given a peculiarly private and internal treatment. Her seven major works and numerous lesser ones all form one immense autobiography. When she began writing, at about fifty, the main mystical terms – rapture, elevation, ecstasy, transport, flight of spirit – were all in a jumble: 'I mean that these different names all refer to the same thing, which is also ecstasy.' In time she came to believe, together with her most eminent disciple and co-worker St John of the Cross and in fact most mystical writers, that the soul's highest realization was not in ecstasy but in obedience, the habitual conformity of the individual will to the divine will. Yet ecstasy did not therefore cease to be the most intense and blissful of transcendent conditions. Indeed mysticism played a part, a large part, in the Counter-Reformation movement as a whole. Where was its vital centre? Rome, Trent, or Spain? Who were its instigators and strategists? And what was Teresa's role in the movement?

Though Rome remained the centre of church authority, the Spanish, at home, elsewhere in Europe, and on three other continents, gave more energy and leadership to the Counter-Reformation than any other people. What has recently been spoken of as the Spanish 'genius for excess' came out in forms of expression ranging from the most extreme mysticism to the most mud-spattered, mundane 'good works.' The passion, and the intolerance, of the Inquisition was characteristically Spanish. In the eyes of one Spanish historian the Inquisition was more Catholic than the Pope and it created on the Iberian peninsula a national Church whose head was the King and whose ruling prelate was the Grand Inquisitor.[5] Without the Spanish Jesuits the Council of Trent may have failed, or its decisions may not have been turned into deeds. In achieving the goals of reforming the Church from within, combating the threat of Protestantism from without, and expanding the Church to foreign lands, the Counter-

Reformation got its impetus primarily from Spain, and within the borders of that land which was just then becoming a nation, the most active and efficacious agent of reform was Teresa of Ávila.

Innate spiritual fervour only partly accounts for the tremendous vigour the Spanish brought to the work of reform. In this, the heyday of her history, Spain's exceptional good fortune was also responsible. After centuries of slumber Spain bestirred herself, and soon became the most powerful figure on the world scene. The rejuvenation began in 1492, Spain's *annus mirabilis* when Columbus set off for the New World and started the flow of wealth from the colonies, and when the Moors, after nearly eight centuries of domination, were driven off the peninsula and Granada was reconquered. At last the Spanish kingdoms were joined under one ruler, and for a time Spain's imperial strength controlled the Low Countries, large parts of what is now Italy, some of North Africa, Portugal and her colonies, and vast territories in the Indies and Americas. It was an empire greater than any since the Roman. 'Had there been more world,' sang the epic voice of Camoëns, 'they would have reached it.'

The span of time which embraces Teresa's lifetime (1515-1582) and extends down to the next century was Spain's greatest. Her power and prestige were never stronger, and her influence, spreading across Europe and beyond it, affected everything down to fashions in food, dress, and language. In due time, when the empire already showed signs of crumbling, the *siglo de oro* began, the Golden Age of Spanish arts and letters which lasted not one century but nearly two. Her culture, never so detached from the rest of Europe as people used to imagine, in the seventeenth century developed into the full flowering of Spanish Baroque – as late a development in Spain as it was in northern and central Europe. After El Greco came Velázquez, Ribera, Zurbarán, Murillo, also Cervantes, Lope de Vega, Calderón, and the poets. After the music of Encina and Narvaez came that of Victoria for the churches. In sculpture Montañés and Cano stand out, and in architecture, which developed last, the Churrigueras and Narciso Tomé.

When the Council of Trent convened in 1545 Teresa was a rather neurotic and purposeless nun of thirty. Some years before, the Capuchins, in order to revive the simple, severe rule of St Francis, had broken with the mother order of Franciscans, and just previously, the Jesuit order was founded by Ignatius Loyola and Francis Xavier, both Spanish Basques. As chief architect of the internationally powerful order, Ignatius worked in Rome, while Francis Xavier went off to Japan and the Indies. Another Spanish Jesuit, Francis Borgia, who was part of the time in Spain where he knew Teresa, worked for the reform chiefly in France and the Indies. Philip Neri who established the Oratorian system for secular priests, was (with Carlo Borromeo) among the few Italians who figured eminently in the Counter-Reformation movement. In fact about half of the thirty-odd saints from the Counter-Reformation period belonged to Spain and her territories.[6] On the memorable day in 1622 when Pope Gregory XV canonized five saints at one time, one, Philip Neri, was Italian and the others, Ignatius Loyola, Francis Xavier, Teresa of Ávila, and Isidore of Madrid (from an earlier time), were all Spanish. We recognize, however, that not all who are saintly become saints, and that the vitality of the Counter-Reformation was not limited to the leaders but expressed itself wherever the ardent work went on, not only in Spain but Italy, France, Poland, Chile, China, the Indies, and elsewhere. In the unity of its purpose and the extent of its effect, the release of energy was a unique phenomenon in Christian history.

One manifestation of the movement was a new attitude toward saints and sainthood. Almost without exception, those who later became saints were active workers in the reform. In a limited way, contemplative discipline had always been directed to useful work, but now, particularly in Spain, spiritual virtues and practical virtues were brought into the closest accord. To explain this condition writers have sometimes found one leading trait of the Spanish character to be sufficient: the heroic instinct which rejects the abstract and theoretical and is forever searching for noble action (this is what Unamuno identifies as Spanish 'ideophobia'). The Spanish mystics were disinclined to go down the misty, iridescent path of Ruysbroeck or to take the ultra-ascetic course of Origen, Athanasius, and the other Alexandrians. Don Quixote stands for the general truth that a Spaniard expresses his ideal not in theory but action. Time and again Spanish writers make clear that the soul's work is measured by the object it chooses to love. The Spaniard seeking a motive for action found it in Divine Love. It was the perfect motive for expressing personal independence, righteous rage, ideals of justice, indeed all the moral needs felt by Spaniards ever since Seneca in the first century. At long last a man's individual will could be fulfilled by the will of God within him.

Thus there came into being a kind of mysticism peculiar to Spain, a new mysticism of action, and with it came a new concept of the saint as worldly leader. Born to believe and to act, the Spanish saints, in God's name, served the world in unusually practical ways. Their *contemptus mundi* was diminished by their loving God passionately in his creatures and creation. These figures, no less than Charles V, had a powerful influence on the Catholic countries. But the issue of faith was by no means their concern alone. The call was heard by large segments of Spanish society. Everyone was urged to subordinate personal interests to the work of religious renewal. Young men and women rushed into clerical life with the same zeal and in the same numbers as the young suitors of Leandra, in Cervantes' fiction, rushed to the countryside to become shepherds.

Since contemplation has seldom become action in the long but broken history of mysticism, an old paradox may have been resolved in Teresa's Spain. Action, far from being antagonistic to the mystical life, nourished and strengthened it. A certain truth resides in Émile Mâle's exaggerated assertion that 'ecstasy became the culmination of Christian life and the supreme effort of art,' but at the same time official authority, in the name of action, firmly resisted the frequent ecstatic spectacles of the day. While Philip III required strict conformity of worship to meet the advances of Protestantism, he was very sternly opposed to all forms of supernatural experience. In fact a mood of scepticism ran through the general population, in part because many mystical events proved to be false. But scepticism existed only because the mystical temper was so strong. One hears on good authority that mysticism is the true centre of Spanish Christianity. Mysticism thrived then as perhaps it never has in any other place or time in the West. The number of mystics then in Spain was so great that the question arises of whether or not mysticism can spread epidemically, isolated cases like St Augustine's notwithstanding.[7] Unquestionably the experience of reaching the divine essence, of being in direct contact with deity, is personal and private. Yet it is equally certain that mystics somehow affect one another. Were this not so, we would be at a loss to explain, for example, the vast and influential literature of mysticism which has been read, as well as written by mystics. Indeed we can see that mystical experience is in different ways both solitary and communicable, if we distinguish between genuine, original mystical experience and the epidemic mystical events commonly believed to be caused by hysteria.

Not surprisingly, in Teresa's era the harvest of mystical writing in Spain was extraordinarily large. Menéndez y Pelayo cannot be right in saying that three thousand mystical works, in print or manuscript, still survive from that day, but even now one can read some twenty mystical writers of the era, and half of them are still being read.[8] The mystical events they seek to describe are contained within the Aquinas definition *cognitio dei experimentalis*, knowing God through experience. These writers try to feel and see the object of their love. They seek immediacy. That they do not always succeed depends partly on the fact that the highest forms of ecstasy (as we shall see) are not directly sensory. But in the effort they express not states of mind but states of the soul and senses. There is the world, which they would restore and make divine. And there is heaven, the soul's final life which cannot now be experienced eternally but can, at moments, be experienced supernaturally.

Teresa herself was simultaneously that individual mystic who springs from the soil spontaneously, and a communicator of mystical experience who affected others and was affected by them. She illustrates so many kinds of connection with others that one is tempted to see her as the focal personality among the mystical writers of the age. Perhaps we should expect as much, considering her geographical location in the centre of the country, the network of Toledo-Madrid-Escorial-Ávila-Segovia-Valladolid-Salamanca-Burgos – in short, Castile. To be sure, she was directly and indirectly associated with hundreds of people in the reform, through talk, work, letters, and published books. And she was in some manner associated with nearly all the important writers of Spain's Golden Age of mysticism. Luis de León and Luis de Granada influenced her thinking, though far less than the brilliant Franciscan priest, Francisco de Osuna. Very likely she studied St Ignatius' *Spiritual Exercises* (as her earliest biographer Ribera says) since it was the outstanding manual of discipline the age produced. Also she knew and worked with St John of the Cross, and was a close friend and confidante of St Peter of Alcántara the seasoned Franciscan writer and reformer. Then there were those she continued to influence after her death. Not only did St John carry on her work but Juan de los Ángeles disseminated her teachings and Luis de León became her first editor.[9]

In her own books Teresa was one of the few who achieved considerable success in describing the most sublime spiritual states, and the achievement places her in the company of such mystical writers as St Augustine, Meister Eckhart, Henry Suso, Jan van Ruysbroeck, St Catherine of Siena, and in the Counter-Reformation period, St John of the Cross. In Teresa's case a fortunate convergence of environment and individual personality produced writing which in some respects excels that of all the others. In writing as in painting, the sixteenth-century artist became overtly a part of his own work. He is the creator and the created, both outside and inside the work. Montaigne himself is the subject of his book, but before he wrote, Teresa had begun to study self-experience minutely and explicitly, and still earlier, other Spanish mystics had also done so, with indifferent success. Among important writers of Europe it is she who set a new standard in the writing of direct, detailed self-revelation. One modern authority on Spanish literature even contends that we know St Teresa more intimately and completely than any other human being before the eighteenth century.[10]

The impulse to start anew, the need or desire to deal intimately and internally with experience was felt by others than Teresa, and in other lands than Spain. A feeling of refreshment was in the spiritual atmosphere and it was this same need or desire which inspired the Council of Trent almost from the beginning. The general will to renew the practice of faith and revise the government of the Church soon prevailed over false starts, papal reluctance, a stubborn Curia, and the tepid attitude of the Emperor. The persistent goadings of Protestants within the Council, as well as outside, did not fail in their effect. Even in the first session which opened with only thirty-four in official attendance, but quickly increased to well over two hundred, the Council's work began in earnest.

With reference to Teresa, the Council's importance is twofold: in its judgments concerning the sacrament of the Eucharist; and closely connected with that, its directives concerning religious art. As the central sacrament of Christian life it was a sharp point of controversy in the Reformation period generally. Partly in reaction to Zwingli's effort to reduce its significance, and to Luther's doctrine of consubstantiation, the Council gave its answer. It determined to re-establish the sacrament of the Eucharist as the primary act of worship, the *mysterium mysteriorum*. As in early Christian centuries it was brought home to believers that the union of God and man re-enacted in Holy Communion was not the symbolic but *actual* consuming of Christ's body and blood. The Council plainly declared that 'a conversion takes place of the whole substance of the wine into the substance of His blood,' and the whole substance of the bread into Christ's material body. At the moment of conversion the bread and wine, though retaining their appearances, become *in substance* the flesh and blood of Christ. By reinterpreting the dogma of transubstantiation in this basic way, the Council quickened the mystical tradition which had been essential to the Catholic faith from the start. The sacramental act was made new. While in the Middle Ages it was usual to receive Holy Communion once a year, now all at once many received it daily.

Where religious art is concerned the Council's directives put controls on both the choice and treatment of a subject, and in some cases also on design – for instance, even though centrally planned churches continued to be built, the plan was condemned as pagan.[11] Especially at the beginning the strict rules were strictly applied, and the effect was often inhibiting. But at the same time, the artist was permitted, virtually encouraged, to express himself with freedom and intensity, as long as the work of art was genuinely religious in purpose. Thus the effect of the directives was also stimulating and liberating. Of course no close and comprehensive evaluation of the Council's influence on art can ever be made. But changes did occur. For the first time Christ or the saints were to be depicted in the full vividness of their agony, their wounds, and their tears. Here was born what has often since then been called 'the new realism' of that era. Emotional and spiritual intensity were meant to be felt. Dramatic and climactic scenes appeared in abundance. Émile Mâle has pointed to the great difference between the relative passiveness in medieval paintings of saints, and the active, engaged appearance of those painted in the seventeenth century. Exceptions aside (one thinks of active Romanesque and Gothic figures, and of prettily passive *seicento* figures, even in Italy), medieval saints, as they read, meditate, heal the sick, kill a dragon, or await death, are quiet in demeanour and facial expression by comparison with seventeenth-century saints who are frequently shown in the climactic moments of their lives. Even Renaissance depictions of a figure like St Sebastian commonly express pious resignation to pain rather than the inner feelings of pain or blissful suffering. The new figures, far from being disembodied spirits, are people living in crisis, divinely touched yet living in the flesh, aware of the earth and of their inward experience.

With the Eucharistic Communion officially interpreted as the *actual* consuming of Christ's body and blood, many new works of art revealed body and spirit in a high degree of unity. The body is now more human and palpable, the spirit more intensely sublime. This does not mean that the new forms of religious art were necessarily superior to the old, but that the Council's instructions enforced or fostered a view of art which aspired to this unity of being. Man in the flesh cannot attain that unity, yet he may experience something close to it, if briefly and imperfectly. An enormous number of Counter-Reformation paintings, especially in Jesuit churches, take the Eucharist out of the context of the Mass and focus directly on the Sacred Host (the wafer) or show saints in adoration before the Eucharist. The reality Teresa herself pictures in her writing is a unified state in which Creator and created exist together: man's body and spirit occupied by Christ's body and spirit, or striving to rise to Christ's body and spirit. There is much truth in the observation that in this era the real subject of religious art was Christ's impact on the individual soul, the human, suffering Christ embodying Godhead.

In describing body and spirit as one, the Spanish mystics therefore renewed a literary tradition which, although in desuetude for long periods of time, was nearly as old as the Church itself. Whatever the differences between the individual writers, this was the starting point. More broadly speaking, it is also the basis on which one may reasonably call much art of the *siglo de oro* 'mystical realism'. The Mannerist idiom soon wore out. In the Prado *Resurrection* El Greco showed a Christ whose internal serenity spreads and falls on the violent world like a veil of peace. But the emotion is artificial and the technique strained, in contrast to the new Spanish idiom of 'mystical realism.' Paintings by Ribera and Zurbarán are dark scenes relieved by luminous faces, broken by gaps of bright light. Their figures may be coarse, haggard, a little mad – Ribera's sudden and violent, Zurbarán's still and contemplative – but they are, in the end, convincing, earth-engendered figures at least half in union with deity.

When Teresa was sainted in 1622 images of her immediately began to appear all over Catholic Europe, in Carmelite convents and churches especially. Her likeness was to be seen in innumerable paintings, prints, statues, and reliefs; events from her life were set to music and put into words. Surprisingly, only one contemporary likeness of her survives, and no major Spanish artist is known to have painted her, although Ribera, Zurbarán, and Murillo all may have, and dozens of minor painters must have, in the course of the seventeenth century.

Among foreign artists who painted her, Lanfranco, Guercino, Tiepolo, Lebrun, Van Dyck, and Rembrandt are the most notable. Since the Bull of Canonization attracted attention to two mystical events of her life, it is natural that one of them, the one Teresa herself describes in a famous account, should be frequently represented in art. It is Teresa's vision of a seraph piercing her heart with a flaming spear. Traditionally said to have occurred on 27 August, 1559, that mystical event has on that day been celebrated annually in Spain for two hundred and fifty years.[12] Aside from its representation in other forms of art, it is the subject of nearly forty paintings, by, among others, Palma Giovane, Calandrucci, and Piazzetta in Italy, and in the north, Pierre Mignard, Rubens, and Gerard Seghers.[13] Regardless of medium, however, there are two versions of the seraphic vision which stand above all others: the poetry of the English 'Metaphysical' Richard Crashaw, and the chapel of Gianlorenzo Bernini. Though the poetry is less immediate and less popular, it ranks with the best mystical poetry in English, and the Cornaro Chapel, which contains the sculpture of Teresa and the seraph, is perhaps the outstanding piece of sculpture of seventeenth-century Rome in one of Rome's most illustrious chapels. The only rival to these two presentations of the visionary event is Teresa's own.

About twenty-three years after she made her profession of vows, there appeared to Teresa this vision of a seraph with his fire-tipped dart. It was one of the first in the series of visions she had between about 1555 and 1580 soon before her death. Some three years after the vision occurred she was instructed by her superiors to write her autobiography, later called the *Vida de Santa Teresa de Jesús*, which includes her account of it. The manuscript of the *Vida*, in her own hand and bound in crimson velvet, is in the library of the Escorial. It had been finished in 1565 and was published posthumously in 1588.

The history of the *Vida* was only begun with that edition. In the next fifty years about ten other editions appeared in Spain, as well as those in Italy, Belgium, and other countries. And it was translated into seven languages. The *Vida* and its companion piece the *Castillo Interior*, which she wrote ten years later, are commonly regarded as classics in the literature of Spain. Among prose works of the Golden Age the *Vida* had a status not far below *Don Quixote* and *Lazarillo de Tormes*, and today too, it is quite widely read in Spain.

Naturally much lore and legend accumulated around the name of Teresa after her canonization. Undoubtedly Bernini and Crashaw knew about Teresa in that way, but also it is likely that Bernini read the *Vida* in Italian, and it is certain that Crashaw read it in Spanish. There resulted one of the most revealing artistic coincidences of the age. Working in different countries and different art media, these two men produced almost simultaneously, late in the 1640's, entirely independent interpretations of St Teresa. Both are leading examples of baroque style: in fact both helped to bring the style into being. The resemblances they have in common, and share with Teresa's original, make a revealing chapter in the cultural history of the Counter-Reformation era.

Two

From Conflict to Accomplishment

If the *Vida* were written as a sustained narrative the seraphic vision might well be its climax. But it is another kind of work, a spiritual autobiography. Its loosely ordered parts sketch in Teresa's spiritual life until she is fifty. Externally speaking, very little happens. Instead the *Vida* traces the transformation of a wilful, rather hysterical girl into a likable, sympathetic, and saintly woman. If all her works comprise an autobiography the *Vida* is the beginning and basis which the others serve mainly to extend and refine. At first Teresa hoped to keep the work anonymous, but the hope soon had to be abandoned. Copies were made and circulated before it was published, and Teresa, to forestall trouble with the Inquisition, invited certain well-informed people to read it, in particular Father Domingo Báñez, a Dominican professor of theology. Despite the precautions, the work got into the hands of the Inquisitors and was denounced. Though the details are not clear, in the end Father Báñez made some small changes, submitted the work to the Inquisitors himself, and approval was given. From that moment the Inquisition not only sanctioned publication but encouraged its distribution.

What was published in 1588 is a profoundly personal account of herself. Though God is central, the woman who seeks him and speaks to him is authentic and persuasive. The chronology is dim. The pages are almost bare of names, dates, and circumstances. Teresa moves among people who though nameless and faceless have definite personalities; she goes to places which though featureless are often identifiable; and she participates in a life with God who though invisible seems to be immediately and personally present.

Possibly she is the first modern woman to become an eminent writer, certainly she is the first to write a personal chronicle. One might imagine

it to follow the line begun by Augustine's *Confessions*, but the resemblance
to Augustine is very slight. It is Teresa's mixed background which leads
Américo Castro to associate the *Vida* with the 'pure inner experience'
of many Arabic works from 1200 and earlier. In his opinion it is impossible to account for the *Vida* solely in terms of the Christian tradition of
'corpo-spiritual mysticism.'[14] What arrests his attention is the spiritual
role of woman that stands out in both the *Vida* and early Islamic, rather
than Christian, literature. There is a difference, however: in her spiritual
role (she has others too) Islamic woman is conceived of as an ideal and
example, while Teresa conceives of herself primarily as a spiritual guide
in the world. Her debt to that tradition may in fact be negligible. In any
case, before Teresa no Spanish writer was concerned to show the effect of
one soul on another, one life on another. Teresa's 'pure inner experience' may allow the phenomenal world almost to dissolve and fade, but the
social motive persists and sensory reality is at no point fully obliterated.

A born writer, Teresa composed swiftly – *a vuela pluma* – and seldom
revised. She writes with the vigour characteristic of Carmelite writers
and with the copiousness of Spanish prose in general, but she has a special
talent for going directly to the heart of an idea. In telling a tale (one of her
well-known gifts) she puts the central point in perfect focus. Fervent
spiritual eloquence is a quality her prose has in common with the poetry
of St John of the Cross, but other qualities are uniquely her own – the
easy spontaneity, the sudden changes in pace and mood, the immediacy
of words which seem suddenly to be born out of an insatiable human
curiosity.[15]

At the same time, however, this eminent writer is no writer. Her books
are no more than the by-products of an active life.

> For the love of God, let me work at my spinning-wheel and
> go to choir and perform the duties of the religious life, like
> the other sisters. I am not meant to write: I have neither the
> health nor the intelligence for it.

She complains also that she lacks the learning, memory, and time to
write. As a rule she wrote whenever and wherever it was possible, beside
the road or amidst the clatter of pots and pans in some convent kitchen.
In fact the *Vida* is exceptional among her works for having been com-

pletely revised, and for having been written, in its last version, not when she was on the move but at St Joseph's in Ávila during 'the most restful years of my life.' The unusual intimacy and zest of the *Vida* surely owes something to these circumstances. Yet even this work closes with a demur:

> I have ventured to put together this story of my unruly life, though I have wasted no more time or trouble on it than has been necessary for the writing of it, but have merely set down what has happened to me with all the simplicity and truth at my command.

We could protest against the casualness with which she refers to these primary virtues, yet the words may point to the very qualities which have attracted readers to her for four centuries: the simplicity of her clear, incandescent language, the truth of her exacting descriptions of spiritual states. She can lead the reader where she will. The *je ne sais quoi* of her style may be its unexceptionable humanness, the same humanness which makes the *Vida* read as a flow of experience, for it is not so much an architectural form as a rushing current of meaning.

The forty chapters arrange themselves into four fairly distinct groups: early life in Ávila (1-10); 'the four waters' which is a widely-known treatise on the stages of prayer (11-22); a section on visions and other phenomena of the mystical life, which is a personal interpretation of 'the four waters', (23-32); and last, an account of the founding of the first Carmelite house, St Joseph's, which closes with a quasi-epilogue on the soul's fulfilment in death (33-40).

The unprotective way in which Teresa examines her life begins with the opening words: 'if I had not been so wicked it would have been a help to me that I had parents who were virtuous and feared God. . . .' The evil and laxity of the world impress themselves on her very early. With her favourite brother (probably Rodrigo) there was much talk and reading about saints and martyrs, and when she was six or seven and he eleven they decided to leave home and seek martyrdom among the Moors. The plan came to nothing, and it receives barely a half-page of space in the *Vida*, yet it quickly became part of her legend. It comes into virtually every biography of Teresa (of which there are over eighty) and also appears prominently in Crashaw's treatment of her. It stands of course as the earliest proof of Teresa's passionate desire to suffer for Christ and attack his enemies. But the really important event of her early life was the death of her mother in Teresa's fourteenth year. It was then that she began to turn away from the world, more specifically from temptations in the life of Ávila – the malicious pleasure of gossip, the vanities of dress, coiffure, and perfume, the idle escapism of chivalric books. But as we shall see in Crashaw, the manner and direction of her life were not clear for a long time to come, not then, not at sixteen when she went briefly to an Augustinian convent in Ávila, not even at twenty-one when she became a novice in the Carmelite Convent of the Incarnation.

The impression one has of her then, gathered mainly from her own words, is of someone strong-willed and intelligent, yet at the same time unsettled, downcast, and quite sickly. But the first half of her life is not well known. Features of the early sketch can be seen in the full-length portrait, however, even though parts of it have been distorted by pious embellishments in many of the biographies. Many thought her beautiful in both body and face, and everyone found her gay, talkative, sharp-minded, endlessly energetic, and unusually generous and good-tempered. There are signs in her own writing that she suffered fools none too lightly and disliked gloomy and ill-tempered people, but she believed in acceptance and told her nuns that the holier they became the more friendly and sociable they had to be. That she was playful and witty seems certain, and that she laughed easily, was fond of dancing, singing (though she joked about having no voice), and playing on the tambourine. Teresa always loved music and found it so worth while a part of religious life that she introduced it into the reformed order, into both the daily recreation periods and the recitation of daily offices.[16]

Perhaps because we know much more about the second half of her life it is harder to picture her as novice, student, or even contemplative, than as a nun riding on the road in her primitive wooden cart, or tramping with her sisters on the rutty, rocky paths of Castile. One episode from her travels has been told many times, and in many forms, since no certain source for it has yet been found. Very possibly it happened on the road near Burgos late in her life.[17] Quite plump and much bent over by hard work, she used to move about with a stick, very swiftly and surely. On this occasion as she rode on a mule she came to a stream in full spring-flood which had to be forded. 'The Lord who helped us through the mud will help us across the river,' she declared. With that she went straight into the river ahead of the others, and soon found herself floating downstream, her habit spread out on the surface of the water. Thrashing wildly about, she began to make for the other side. Finally reaching it, no more alive than dead, she promptly knelt down to thank God for her survival. 'Dear Lord,' she said, 'is this the way you treat us who love you and work for you?' When the Lord replied, 'Yes', Teresa answered, 'Then that may be why we are so few.'

It may be important that we have so indistinct an idea of Teresa's appearance yet so clear an idea of her personality. Apparently there survives only one contemporary likeness of her, the mediocre painting by Juan de la Miseria in Valladolid. It conveys so little that one is more inclined to compare her with a figure carved by Gregorio Fernández, realistic in colour and modelling yet hauntingly illusionistic, or a Murillo portrait, bathed in blue-tinted light, supremely spiritual but also sensuous and entirely feminine.

When the young Teresa took vows at the Convent of the Incarnation in Ávila she did so with no special conviction. There was no lack of sincerity or piety, yet one is aware that young people drifted into convents and monasteries as in other times they drift into marriage, the professions, or civil service. Spain then had some nine thousand active religious houses and a third of the population worked in the service of the Church. There is much ironic truth in the comment that Castile produced mystics in large numbers because its people had so little to renounce. Beyond personal and social circumstances, the physical environment of Ávila must have affected Teresa. It was like an acropolis on the hilltop, its slopes strewn with granite boulders. In November the grey light and towered walls of the city must have given the scene a sense of over-whelming grandeur and severity. Many years after, Teresa's personal explanation was that she entered the convent 'inspired by fear' rather than love. It is a comment of much poignancy since her long spiritual struggles began at this time: 'I spent nearly twenty years on that stormy sea.' Though preferring the convent to home, the life was disturbing in many ways. She felt completely unworthy of it. Even when she heard the narrative of Christ's Passion she could not weep freely and genuinely as the other nuns did. Her belief that a convent should never be a place of escape did not make existence any easier. In her opinion those who went there to escape from the world were rewarded by finding themselves 'in ten worlds at once.' She had no real equilibrium of her own, however. 'I seemed to have trampled the world beneath my feet,' was her response at one moment, and at the next she chastises herself for being 'a whole seaful of evils' (*piélago de los malos*).

Although Teresa's respect for learning lasted long after she gave up the habit of reading, in her twenties particularly she read and studied intensively. Now, in contrast to chivalric romances, she says, 'I loved reading good books.' The Bible and saints' lives were of course daily fare in the convents. The books of the Bible she liked best were those generally favoured then, the Psalms, the Song of Songs, and the Gospels of Matthew, Luke, and John. Beyond these she also read widely in the Spanish mystics, and in Augustine, Jerome, Gregory the Great, Ludolph of Saxony, and probably Vincent Ferrer.[18]

Later on, even though she continued writing books all her life, Teresa began to resist them. Her itinerant way of living certainly discouraged reading. Also, after the *Index Librorum Prohibitorum* was issued in 1559, only Latin books could be read and Teresa knew very little Latin. Like all women of the day she had no formal education. The fact that the only Bibles available to her were in Latin must have severely impaired even her reading of that; it helps, however, to clear up the mystery of how a person with her immense knowledge of the Bible could have made references to it which were so often vague or wrong. By necessity she gained that knowledge by other means, not the least of which were her countless conversations with the learned, for she habitually sought out bishops, priests, and laymen for knowledge and advice, and she questioned them tirelessly. While it is true that Teresa was much more learned than most women of the age, she was hardly a Renaissance polymath. On the contrary, she distrusted all knowledge not drawn from direct experience, and also believed that reading could distract her and others from meditation and good acts. At one point she forbade her nuns to learn Latin. At another she said to a girl who wanted to bring her Bible into the convent, 'Bible, child? You shall not come here then . . . for we are ignorant women, and we do nothing but spin and obey.' Ultimately books were among the 'things' Teresa learned to reject. The Bible is the one book to which her writing shows deep indebtedness. All the others, aside from faint impressions and scattered references, were little more than traces lost in the immensity of her work.[19]

During the many years spent in the Convent of the Incarnation one kind of experience shaped Teresa's character more than any other. It was illness – illness and other afflictions. Because of her unpathetic tone it is hard to believe that she was unwell almost all the time between adolescence and her forty-fifth year, plagued by heart trouble, fainting fits, tumours, broken bones, catalepsy, and smaller distresses like ulcerated teeth and a morning nausea which lasted quite steadily for twenty years. 'Sometimes I felt as if sharp teeth had hold of me, and so severe was the pain they caused that it was feared I was going mad.' One illness nearly destroyed her. A four-day cataleptic seizure left her 'doubled up like a ball,' so helpless that she had to be carried around in a sheet, and so paralysed that at first she could move only one finger of one hand. The paralysis lasted three years, but when the disease first attacked it was thought to be fatal. Extreme unction was given, an open grave prepared, and the nuns kept a death-watch. According to Ribera, when her father came to the convent he was told that Teresa was dead and that he should give consent for the burial. For some reason he was not convinced and refused to give it. From Teresa's point of view there was no doubt at all that the nuns believed she was dead: 'afterwards I actually found some wax on my eyelids.'

When the crippled, sickly figure of Teresa mended itself and she became erect and well the change was considered a miracle. For a time she was a sort of sacred specimen used to raise funds for the convent. Primarily, however, something more complicated was happening. Perhaps none of her illnesses and afflictions were purely physiological. In a typically modern way (though the Greeks also knew about psychosomatic symptoms) Teresa understood that there were psychological and spiritual implications too. Her life was a daily dying; her experience was a series of 'little deaths,' an apprenticeship in pain during which she was acutely conscious of Christ's suffering. The oscillations between something like life and death seemed to be a discipline for the extraordinary spiritual conditions she would experience later. It was as if the first half of her life was spent in training the body to be subject to the soul in the second.

By the time she wrote the *Vida* Teresa was sure she had been reborn. 'By this distress,' she once remarked, 'the soul is purified, worked upon and refined like gold in a crucible.' As the Castilian proverb says, the earth and its people conceive and yield out of agony. Her own words come out not with tragic resonance but with awe and relief. As it dawns on her that 'the Lord seems to have raised me from the dead, I am so amazed that inwardly I am almost trembling.' The physical phenomena only deepen the spiritual – just as in ecstasy the body's involvement with the spirit only intensifies the experience. The reality of Teresa's belief that she was reborn lay in the fact that when she was forty-four or forty-five she became well and stayed well until the last years of her life. At about that time other things also changed: her mystical life began, her plans for conventual reform were conceived, and her first book was written.

Strangely enough, however, her good health did not immediately advance her spiritual progress. Recovery only presented her with the choice of following God's way or the world's way. She loved company, talked engagingly, and not only inquired but listened, because she was concerned. Her vigorous activity on their behalf is one reason why for a year and a half she completely gave up 'spiritual prayer.' That kind of silent praying had for centuries been a central part of Carmelite worship. Almost the worst period of spiritual 'aridity' in her life came just then. For the time being the world's way prevailed.

After that phase passed, the feeling of a new life did indeed come over her. Everything she says and does veins out from Christ. Life acquires a certainty it never had before. Her mood is often elated, generally lively and contented – though not steadily, since one who is constantly aware of Christ's wounds and models her life on Christ's cannot rest easy for long. Yet a new quickness of spirit and sharpness of mind is evident even in her letters (which are among the best in any age or country), and she now enjoys the 'gift of tears' she previously lacked. Among the visions which began to come to her, one – which Bernini depicts in the vault of his chapel – is of Christ saying to her, 'Behold this nail. It is a sign that from today onward thou shalt be my bride.'[20]

Like almost any nun in any era Teresa had begun to anticipate her

Mystical Marriage with Christ – who in Crashaw's poetry is her 'fair spouse' and 'sov'reign spouse'. In time her involvement with Christ's life developed so far that her own trials were not *for* him but *in* him. The theme of the marriage goes on through the next twenty-five years and in the last Holy Communion of her life she addresses 'my bridegroom and my saviour.'

Teresa's view of books is informative once more, now in a different way. Finally, after eighteen years of effort, she is able to meditate without holding a book 'like a bait to my soul.' Books, as object, lose more and more of their reality, until Teresa concludes that only three are worthy of attention: the Bible, the 'book of nature,' and the greatest of the three, Christ himself, 'the book in which I have seen what is true.'

Teresa reads the book of nature like a neo-Platonist, or like those sixteenth-century poets and painters who saw meanings *through* nature. She never looks very directly even at water, for which she had a genuine fondness. To her, 'nature' signifies everything God created, and whatever she looks at reminds her of the Creator. Thus the great natural forces, fire and water, are primarily metaphors, and birds, bees, butterflies, and other lesser creatures are smaller metaphors. Birds are souls darting in space, vainly searching for an earthly resting place; and fire is a dozen things, all of them deriving from the original fire of Divine Love.

Books and writing were always subordinate to the work of building the new Carmel, the Spanish Carmel composed of faithful people living devoutly and usefully. The first step was the long struggle to found the house of St Joseph's at Ávila, the first of the Carmelite reform and the first anywhere to be dedicated to St Joseph. Others would follow, small, simple, rudely furnished, but sufficient for the thirteen nuns or monks that each house was intended to hold. In these was re-established the 'Primitive Rule' of the order which was traditionally believed to have begun with Elijah in Palestine twenty-five centuries before, primarily the rule of poverty, labour, and silence.

According to Teresa's account, she had not been unhappy in the Convent of the Incarnation and it was not inferior to other houses of the order. Her chief complaint was that so much of the work she was summoned to do was outside the convent that it seriously interfered with a life of prayer, meditation, and simple labours shared with the other sisters. But the difference between that house and St Joseph's must have been enormous. The Bull of Mitigation issued in 1432 had by official order relaxed the government of all Carmelite houses. This one, which housed one hundred and eighty nuns and had quite free traffic with the city, was not unlike a residence for young ladies of good breeding; some of the sisters were known to decorate their private oratories to personal taste, to use jewellery and perfume, to remodel their habits according to the fashions, and to give small concerts for which they composed sentimental songs.[21]

As far as we know, the idea of reform began with a remark Teresa casually made to her cousin María de Ocampo. Tentatively at first, Teresa sounded out a few people whom she knew and trusted. It is easy to imagine that if any such scheme were known, the instigator would be charged with insubordination, acts of pride, and more. Teresa proceeded with fear and hesitation, for she was not inclined to circumvent or defy ecclesiastical authority. Her purpose became firm only after 'locutions' with God commanded her to go ahead. She proceeded sometimes hesitantly, sometimes boldly. When it was reported to her that the Inquisition would call her up, her reaction was merely to laugh. Every kind of obstacle had to be faced, countless practical problems, the opposition of Ávila's citizens and officers of the Church, and in addition, grave self-doubts. As she remarked afterwards, 'there was hardly anyone who was not against us and did not consider our project absolutely ridiculous.' On the other hand she had, in addition to divine approval, the support of a few clerics and lay friends, especially Francis Borgia, a Jesuit, the Dominicans Domingo Báñez and Luis de Bertran, and her wise and wizened old friend, the Franciscan friar Peter of Alcántara, a man of martyr-like habits who seemed to Teresa to be 'made of nothing but roots of trees.'

At last, after the papal Bull of Permission was validated, St Joseph's was founded on St Bartholomew's Day, 1562. At the mass celebrating the founding, fifteen people were present including Teresa, Peter of Alcántara, the bishop's representative, and the four novices who took vows that day. It was a plain affair and a plain building. The sleeping neighbourhood must have been surprised to wake to the strange sound of the three-pound cracked bell just installed on top of the house.

Considering Teresa's gift for practical affairs, her sureness of touch, her extraordinary tenacity, and her friendly attraction to priests, peasant women, aristocrats, and scholars, it was perhaps inevitable that she and her sisters would not only found a new house but reform the whole order. After Rubeo, the Carmelite general, was sent by the Pope to inspect St Joseph's, Teresa was quickly given permission and encouragement to found other houses. Rubeo found there, in actuality, exactly what the Council of Trent was about to order in its directives.

After the quiet interlude in St Joseph's, Teresa began travelling over Castile and as far south as Seville and Granada, to establish the Discalced or 'Barefoot' Carmelites whose nuns and monks would later make up the larger part of the order. In Spain alone over sixty houses were founded during Teresa's lifetime, and by the early eighteenth century over two hundred were in active operation, of which half were nunneries. Ultimately there were close to five hundred Carmelite houses in Europe, most of them nunneries, and there were still others in the New World and the Middle East.[22] The work was so hard that in fact the new Carmelites were not literally 'barefoot' but wore hemp-soled sandals. Teresa habitually made the best of things, and her talk must often have comforted and inspired the sisters when they were distressed and discouraged. She taught mainly by example, but on occasion gave advice like this:

> . . . try then, sisters, to be as pleasant as you can, without offending God, and go on as well as you can with those you have to deal with, so that they may like talking to you and want to follow your way of life and conversation, and not be frightened and put off virtue. . . . Never keep aloof from them if you wish to help them and to have their love.

The age gradually became more receptive to reform, and in that respect Teresa's life became easier. Both early and late her spiritual ardour never caused her eye to wander far from practical necessities. In her writing the practical life and the inward spiritual life run together. The founding of St Joseph's was the outward and visible expression of the inner life she calls 'the four waters.' In the scheme of the *Vida* those chapters and the succeeding account of visions bring the reader directly up to the vision of the seraph.

Three

The Art of Ascent

In the *Vida* and other mystical works spiritual growth is represented as an ascent through three or four 'degrees of prayer.' These are the stages or phases which Teresa, to expand literal description outwardly by metaphor, gives the name of 'the waters.' The summit of the ascent is invariably the *unión mistica* which in the *Vida* is identical with ecstasy (though we recall that union and ecstasy are not synonymous in her later writing). Ecstasy, if we let one word stand for a cluster of related words, is the state in which man is farthest removed from his normal human condition, the state in which prayer perfectly attains its ideals. It is a moment borrowed from eternity, a foretaste of heaven.

Since in ecstasy we are least like our natural selves – the very word *ek-stasis* is a 'standing outside' oneself – language and empirical verification are both at a disadvantage. Any account of ecstasy suffers from the writer having to be detached from the ecstatic state before he can write, and from having to use a vehicle which, like any other vehicle, is incapable of re-creating the experience accurately and completely. As Teresa says more than once, 'to make any attempt to explain a matter which cannot even begin to be described in words may very well be foolish,' and again, 'we cannot be meant to understand it while we are on earth.' Every conceivable means may be used to close the gap between the word and the thing: memory, intuition, denotative language, and the approximations of metaphor, hyperbole, and paradox, and yet every account we read is marred by one defect or another: opaque subjectivity, distorted objectivity, mistaken tone, imprecision of some sort. At the same time, it may be no exaggeration to say that the writings of St Teresa and St John of the Cross treat mystical states more precisely and systematically than any previous writing, and perhaps any writing later, since the importance of such experience has obviously dwindled. The modern study of mysticism, from Saudreau at the turn of the century to David Knowles today, may be said to use these two saints as its main point of reference. The interest St Teresa and St John took in understanding mysticism comprehensively, objectively, and systematically was symptomatic of the era. Before that, no one had made the attempt. Before they wrote, not even the key terms of mysticism had begun to win common consent.

Although they influenced each other through years of close association, Teresa had nearly finished writing by the time St John began, and their achievements are distinguishable. St John's strength lies in brilliant theoretical exploration and in the clarification of much of the language and many of the formal problems of mysticism. These are the achievements of his prose, particularly in the *Ascent of Mount Carmel* and *Dark Night of the Soul*, as distinguished from the divine lyricism for which his poetry is celebrated. On the other hand, Teresa's strength lies in precise empirical observation, in a language very sensitively tuned to its subject, in her explanation of minute *changes* within the soul – an entirely new inquiry – and in her demonstration of the individual's total involvement in mystical experience, body, mind, and spirit. One's achievement does not excel the other's. Both writers are strongly empirical and neither is a scholar. But their qualities of mind differ. Unlike Teresa, St John was formally trained in theology, and therefore more expert in dealing with the terms and concepts of mysticism. Though her knowledge of the terms certainly advanced later on, when she writes the *Vida* 'ecstasy' is still in solution with 'vision,' 'trance,' 'transport,' 'rapture,' and 'union' itself.[23] 'I am unable to use the proper terms,' she plainly says, 'and I cannot understand what is meant by "mind" or how this differs from "soul" or "spirit." They all seem the same to me, though the soul sometimes issues from itself, like a fire that is burning and has become wholly flame. . . .' Because she confronts this problem squarely she is very little inclined to assign arbitrarily rigid meanings to words. The disciplined empiricism of the approach allows her to isolate various spiritual states, examine them, and to arrange them into a progressive advance culminating in union or the Mystical Marriage. Unlike many medieval writers she is freed from the necessity of erecting a structure and filling it in. Instead she asserts that certain areas of perception are dim and leaves them dim, for it was never her intention to build up a scheme of the mystical life in a perfect and unbroken series of steps, and she was never so unintelligent as to think that the definitions and formulations of mysticism could be final. In the course of twenty years the advance of her knowledge is clearly evident, particularly in her best writing on mysticism, the *Vida*, the *Castillo Interior*, and the fifth of her *Spiritual Relations*, but the *Vida* itself gives a good account of where she is going.

Spanish mystical literature of the sixteenth century was nurtured by many things, including the troubadours, the chivalric novel, and Petrarch's sonnets. Scholars have generally divided it along stylistic lines, according to the uses made of image, metaphor, and the like. No wonder metaphor is important to her. Many examples occur, one of the best known being the *Castillo Interior* where the soul's progress is traced through concentric 'mansions' to God at the centre, but in her writing as a whole it is the metaphors of fire and water which predominate. Yet metaphorical meanings do not exclude literal meanings and the two often fuse – exactly as one might expect from a writer who generally regards heaven and earth, spirit and body, and man and man as continuums. The antipathy and sympathy between fire and water was an old, old story, of course, so that nothing about their antipathy in nature need have prevented Teresa, in picturing total, cosmic reality, from showing the two elements frequently existing together and in harmony. Among the many which they share, the chief likeness, in both literal and metaphorical forms, is movement. It is the basic feature of Teresa's own conception and, as we shall see, of Bernini's and Crashaw's conceptions of her.

Metaphorical meanings aside, water, the less abstract of the two elements, was a physical presence, or absence, for Teresa and every other Castilian. She once says she is more attracted to water than anything else in nature. She remembers it at home as a child, in a picture of Christ (again literal and also more than literal) talking to a Samaritan woman about 'the waters of life' while he rests at a well in a Samaritan town. As the *Vida* unfolds we know water to be the life-giving element, indiscriminately physical and spiritual, which nourishes crops, animals, human bodies, human souls, which cools, cleanses, purifies, and quenches thirst. Indeed Theresa saw its presence everywhere on earth and in the sky.

In the *Vida*, domestic, natural, and spiritual forms of fire and water all have their source in deity. By means of 'the waters' God nourishes the garden of the soul in four ways: first, with water laboriously carried by hand from the well; second, with water raised in larger quantities by water-wheel or bucket-and-windlass; third, with water flowing from a stream or brook; and last, with water falling from heaven in a downpour of rain. The long ascent is uneven and unsure; 'no soul on this road is such a giant that it does not often need to become a child at the breast again.'

In 'the waters' it is not usually the ideas which are memorable, since most of them are familiar or predictable, but the rich individuality of Teresa's treatment of them. In the process of losing its selfhood, its attachment to earthly things, its private consciousness, the soul concentrates on Christ in his suffering. Rigorous self-scrutiny takes the form of comparing one's own little life to Christ's: 'I desire to suffer, Lord, because Thou didst suffer,' Teresa says in 'the first water.' One is kept aware that the objective of 'the waters' is always the discipline of prayer: prayer which is vocal and active in the first degree; in the second more passive, as the 'prayer of Quiet'; and in the third, totally passive, the faculties and consciousness being just barely able to function; while in the fourth and last degree the state of ecstasy is still ahead at the peak of the soul's ascent. Of course few people reach even 'the Quiet' and almost no one the final stages; nor can we surmise how long any change might take, since what happens to one person in six months may require twenty years for another. Through all these changes, objectified and generalized as they are, Teresa is also reiterating her own experience step by step. She judges that she stayed too long in the first stage, being reluctant to give up active, discursive prayer for the deeper states of passive prayer, and she makes clear that the condition of the 'third water,' *un sueño de las potencias* or sleep of the faculties, was something she experienced only five or six years before the time she writes, and after decades of disciplined effort.

The very word 'effort' raises the searching question of how the *will* functions or fails to function in various phases of the soul's progress – a question not made simpler by the frequency with which Teresa uses 'will' and 'soul' interchangeably. Does the will actively pursue its own well-being? Yes. Do benefits therefore come to it? Not necessarily. In other words the will seeking to lose itself in God cannot prevail over God's will; nor, on the contrary, can it merely be idle and wait for good things to happen. It is by nature egotistical and prone to error, and it may, out of boredom, pain, or impatience, act against its own well-being. We are observing a subtle process in which the will tries to become stronger and by becoming stronger becomes less and less itself, until finally it is not itself but part of God's will. We seem to be in a hopeless antinomy, but in actual experience the process works out: prayer disciplines the soul to belong to God. Not all the stages of change are conscious and discernible, however, for the will and other faculties are, in the end, learning how to yield themselves up to God. The pattern is unvarying from its first occurrence in 'the Quiet': the soul desires and pursues the condition, but can attain it only if God grants it. Exactly the same thing is true of ecstasy, the highest condition. No matter how ardently the will *wants* to yield itself up, nothing it can do, no prayer, meditation, or other act of devotion, can cause it to happen. Having no power whatever to induce God to do anything, the will (or soul) can only train itself in 'spiritual preparedness,' in readiness and receptiveness.

Teresa's manner of describing how the will produces nothing without God's help is homely, Castilian, and very characteristic of her: if God wants to give wings to toads he does not wait for them to achieve it by their own effort. The everyday element here is a prominent and persistent feature of her style as of many Spanish styles, and it appears also in the late-Renaissance writing, painting, and sculpture of other European countries. We may associate earthy wit and proverbial truth first of all with Sancho Panza, but it is a distinctly Spanish form of thought.[24] No nation is more in love with mother wit. The everyday, often naturalistic element appeared frequently. The Virgin of Velázquez's *Immaculate Conception* is unmistakably, naturalistically, a Spanish girl, and Murillo's madonnas are not idealized figures but young women from Andalusia. The everyday element in the literature, which drew much of its energy from medieval drama, works its way into Camoëns, Cervantes, Quevedo, and the dramatists, and into the religious writing of Luis de León and St Teresa, among others. In her writing it takes the forms of colloquial talk laden with diminutives, superlatives, vernacular words and phrases, and general informality of manner. Her style, far from being larded with foreign or learned words, sounds as though she is talking face to face with her nuns and Castilian neighbours, digressing, interrupting herself, repeating herself.

If one wonders how such an easy, intimate style can reach up to spiritual sublimity, the answer is that Teresa makes direct contact with spiritual events on every level of consciousness. The style stays whole. Teresa in the convent kitchen is Teresa in the chapel and Teresa in ecstasy. Relatively few writers have the simplicity to define union as 'two different things becoming one' the way she does. Human warmth is in virtually every sentence, yet one recognizes that she is also testing and interpreting her experience as she goes along, and in that process addresses herself simultaneously to the reader, God, and herself. The empirical emphasis may not be stronger than in St John's writing, but he, very differently, removes from his prose all traces of personal experience, and in fact he tells us that Teresa had already dealt with personal mystical experience more effectively than he could. Yet the different parties she addresses are a reminder that she is always trying to verify and generalize her experience, to find in it what is typical and universal – a point also confirmed by the constant shifts she makes among 'I,' 'a person,' 'the soul,' 'one,' 'my will,' and 'we.' That which is uniquely personal is declared to be; the rest, even though the idiom is personal, is always being pushed toward objective validity. As her leading English interpreter says, what Teresa presents is a 'mapping of the normal spiritual progress' – not the exceptional but the normal.[25]

As the spiritual history moves and evolves one is made aware of inner states of the soul. 'What I do seek to explain is the feelings of the soul when it is in this divine union.' Only the satisfactions of strenuous discipline are felt in the first phase (which most mystics call 'recollection') in contrast to 'the Quiet' which follows – a state of sheer delight, though so brief-lived that one feels tender in it, constantly fearing it will end. For a time the feeling of self-consciousness is almost overwhelming. The will seems to be watching its own activity. But in the third degree the self-consciousness disappears and the faculties (the 'will, understanding, and memory' taken from scholasticism) function separately, irregularly, with the result that one is at a loss to express what the condition is like.

The intransigent problem of expression asserts itself strongly here, for this sublime condition is but one degree less sublime than ecstatic union. The soul desires to be all tongue, to sing only God's praises, but it can express nothing sensible and its words, says Teresa in a pun, are no more than *mil desatinos santos*, 'a thousand holy absurdities.'

As Teresa says, she must be deeply immersed in prayer in order to write. Without the condition of prayer she writes gibberish; with it, everything lights up and she writes as if her pen were a needle copying out a pattern clearly laid down before her eyes. There are times, she says, when 'I write as mechanically as birds taught to speak, and if the Lord wishes me to say anything new, His Majesty will teach me.' Of course there is no ultimate clarity concerning the double or mid-condition in which she writes – and indeed *lives*. Higher spiritual states can be lost, or be fitful, but in general they should be thought of not as eccentric moments but conditions of life which have duration. Teresa *lives* in 'the Quiet' and in the third stage is 'in an active and contemplative life at one and the same time,' so that she can meditate, work, pray, write, and do other things while in that condition, *because* in that condition. When writing, she sometimes has so little consciousness that she seems to possess a facility very like 'the gift of tongues': 'I, who understand hardly anything that I recite in Latin . . . have been able to understand the text as though it were in Spanish.' Perhaps her central assertion about this 'third water' is that abundant, excited words of sense and nonsense all pour out of her together to express an inner condition that is 'a glorious folly, a heavenly madness, in which *true wisdom is acquired.*'

On the very threshold of fruition the soul yet falters before giving itself up completely. Almost suspended between heaven and earth – just as Bernini shall represent her in ecstasy – Teresa appears on at least one occasion to be divided internally. A part of her soul seems to be distant from her, 'seen' at a distance, as it were. Teresa refers to that part (or that other aspect of soul) as 'she': '*she* would be glad if *she* could have been cut to pieces . . . ,' while the other part, called 'I' and 'my soul,' stays within her. Pain exists on every level of prayer in fact, and more acutely on the higher levels. Withdrawal from this 'heavenly madness,' causes very sharp distress. Another great pain, much prolonged, is an acute feeling of loneliness. Separation from the earth and people is the cause of pain. Far from Ávila, late in her life, she writes, 'I am extremely lonely here. . . . I find such loneliness in spiritual matters. . . . Indeed, I find loneliness everywhere.' Her self quite lost, her soul all but absorbed in God, she senses removal. Looking down upon the earth, its people, and herself there, she cares very little about all of it. 'I care more about the smallest degree of progress achieved by one single soul.'

The metaphor of water records every change in terms of the soul's relation to grace. At first one gains the capacity to draw up the water of tears from the well of suffering. 'Tears achieve everything: one kind of water attracts another.' Water is produced only by limited, manual means in the first two stages, though in the second (the metaphor now changing) God first places in the soul a divine spark of love, and Teresa has the sense that he is walking in the garden of her soul. After that the water comes in greater abundance, the garden is irrigated by a running stream. Then, in the fourth degree, when one least expects it, the rain comes pouring down from heaven and turns everything into unspeakable bliss. 'Aridity' is gone, and the soul is overcome by a 'rejoicing, unaccompanied by any understanding of the thing in which the soul is rejoicing.'

> If the ground is well dug over by trials, persecutions, back-bitings and infirmities (for few attain such a state without these), and if it [the ground] is broken up by detachment from self-interest, the water will sink in so far that the ground will hardly ever grow dry again.

At this point in the progress another paradox occurs: Teresa's autobiography ceases to be autobiography because she ceases henceforth to write about herself. She had wondered what the soul actually did in God's presence and now she is told: 'it dies to itself, daughter, in order that it may fix itself more and more upon me; it is no longer itself that lives, but I.' In the state of ecstasy the soul is totally absorbed. No self exists outside the ecstasy. The soul in this state has been compared to a bird which cannot see the air which supports it, or a fish which cannot see the water in which it swims. It knows all and knows nothing, yet it feels its condition. The anomaly of pleasure-pain which already appeared on the third level as 'delightful disquiet' and 'delectable pain,' appears at its strongest here, as it will again in Crashaw and Bernini. Surely it is actual and authentic experience. Yet it seems also to be a paradox which attempts to account in words for a condition which is too extreme to describe. The intensity of pleasure-pain comes out in great swirling phrases which in the *Vida*, as in other accounts of mystical life, blur the meanings of the words. Pain may be a delight, and pleasure may be its cause or its consequence. Here the simplest, most frequent expression of pleasure-pain is in paradoxes, though pleasure, or benefit, is dominant in the collective effect. The pain is 'severe enough to kill me . . . yet it is so delectable, and the soul is so conscious of its worth, that it desires it.' 'It is a martyrdom' in which the excess of pain is beyond endurance, but 'I should like to spend the rest of my life suffering in that way.' One form, on more than one level, is the beneficent suffering we associate with sainthood and tragedy, here the *dolor sabroso* ('sweet-tasting suffering') and the 'suffering love' which Unamuno observed in Teresa. Perhaps the pricks or shafts of pain inflicted on pleasure only heighten and sharpen it, even to the point of delirium, and perhaps all mundane experience is a pallid version of celestial experience. In actuality pleasure and pain come not only separately but together. Ultimately the two together yield a product which exceeds the sum of both. A third kind of experience is created which is different from both, not pleasure-pain but a nameless something which we may, in the absence of any word for it, describe as 'bliss.' By its nature this uncommon or unknown third condition is without any definition at all. Yet it may be that this condition, this 'bliss,' is in its highest forms simultaneously excited and peaceful, and that when the faculties are exhausted there remains a sense of total well-being. Such, in any case, are the meanings one can elicit from Teresa's writing.

The soul, in the final paradox of all, is on the point of transcending itself. It is

> not in itself at all, but on the house-top, or the roof of its
> own house, and raised above all created things; I think it is
> far above even its highest part.

Escaping from the earth and the reach of death, it desires only to glorify its Creator. But all at once consciousness may return and break into the blissful condition, at which point the words slacken and go cold, utterly failing to grasp the mystical reality. Again Teresa acknowledges that ecstasy can cut down language in one stroke. 'It is more impossible to say anything about it than to talk Greek. . . . So I laid it aside and went to Communion.'

Four

Seraphic Fire

The two chapters concluding Teresa's account of the 'fourth water' read like a free-form essay on ecstasy. It is really a synthesis of ecstatic experience, her own and also that of others, which tells, quite informally, what ecstasies are like, from the moment of onset to the final after-effects. Here also Teresa keeps the emphasis on 'the feelings of the soul when it is in this divine union.' These chapters and the seven which follow do not come here by chance, however. They make a setting for the seraphic vision described in Chapter 29, and they contain, moreover, the deeply inward meaning which comes out in Bernini and Crashaw. The flaming sword which crowns the official insignia of the Discalced Carmelites is an emblem of spiritual militancy and fervour. It may also be an emblem of Teresa the founder, and a reference to the fiery vision which is the most celebrated event of her mystical life.

What we hear of such experiences is so varied and uncertain that it is surprising to see how much the different kinds of mystical events have in common. The main features of ecstasy, including the seraphic vision, all appear in Teresa's writing. An ecstasy takes hold like a 'powerful eagle, rising and bearing you up with it on its wings.' To resist it is almost impossible, and when it seizes one, body and soul seem to join and co-inhere. Which is which, one cannot always say, nor is it clear whether the soul ever, even for a moment, leaves the body behind during a rapture. 'If the soul is in the body or not while all this is happening I cannot say,' Teresa writes in the *Castillo Interior*, and here: 'I would not myself swear that the soul is in the body, nor that the body is bereft of the soul.' An ecstasy is a rather brief event, as brief as the blink of an eye, or when prolonged, in Teresa's case anyway, it lasts no more than half an hour. The mystic may appear to onlookers to be in ecstasy for three or four hours, but he himself knows that the intensity of it varies greatly and that an ecstasy is only a short interval in what can be a very long period of prayer. 'Again and again God gives more in a moment than in a long period of time.'

Even at the height of a rapture complete loss of consciousness is extremely rare. It is more accurate to say that consciousness takes a new form. In the slow journey from the Many to the One it withdraws from the circumference to the centre, fixing its attention on one thing only. While the ecstasy lasts, the mystic lives in the spiritual world as truly as the average person lives in the sensual. As a rule the body for some reason stays in the position it had when the seizure came on, standing or sitting, sometimes with legs and arms rigid, or fists clenched, as if the transport were outside of time. Most commonly a subject can see nothing, though the eyes may be open or closed. He cannot move or speak yet he can 'hear and understand, but only dimly, as though from a long way off,' hearing without understanding what is heard. And the breathing slows down: 'my pulses almost cease to beat, my bones are all disjointed, and my hands so stiff that sometimes I cannot clasp them together.' In deep raptures the body temperature also falls and the hands sometimes become ice-cold. Since the body's strength seems to decline as the soul's increases, it may be said that a certain kind of separation can occur. But reports differ and not even one individual's experiences are consistent on all occasions, particularly since the faculties of the soul are completely suspended. The soul is conscious mainly of 'fainting almost completely away, in a kind of swoon, with an exceeding great and sweet delight.'

> This last water which we have described is so abundant that, were it not that the ground is incapable of receiving it, we might believe this cloud of great majesty to be with us here on this earth. But as we are giving Him thanks for this great blessing, and doing our utmost to draw near to Him in a practical way, the Lord gathers up the soul, just (we might say) as the clouds gather up vapours from the earth, and raises it up till it is right out of itself . . . and the cloud rises to heaven and takes the soul with it, and begins to reveal to it things concerning the kingdom that He has prepared for it.

I do not know if the comparison is an exact one, but that is the way it actually happens.

Though it is not easily explored, the phenomenon of bodily levitation has bearing on the seraphic ecstasy, less however in the *Vida* than in Bernini's and Crashaw's versions of it. It is an event reported by no fewer than two hundred saints and mystics, and very understandable as part of the subject's experience. Several times Teresa speaks to this effect: 'I could hardly tell when my feet were touching the ground.' Often there are onlookers who confirm the phenomenon, and here the difficulty arises, for there is a difference between apparent objective verification and the fact that nearby figures may be swept up by the all-engrossing power of an ecstasy. Whatever we make of the observers to whom Teresa refers, there is no doubt that she herself felt this sense of weightlessness when in the grip of rapture, or just afterwards.

When the vision passes, body and soul may both suffer terrible agonies. There is the internalized pain the body feels from having its normal functions suspended, and there is the pain the soul feels from losing the bliss of God's immediate presence. It is so severe a shock to be dropped back into the world that re-adjustment frequently requires several days, during which time the external world seems utterly unreal. The painful sense of loneliness may linger on without much chance of relief, because the soul, which wants only to keep its divine yearnings alive, is quite out of touch with the world.

After the mystical event another fear or anxiety appears, in the form of trying to discover whether the ecstasy was genuine. Was it that, a trick of the devil, or a feat of self-hallucination? As time went on Teresa became more experienced in testing genuineness, the basic always being not the vividness or grandeur of the ecstasy but its effects. While she can sense this by self-observation, there is always something to be gained by referring the experience to learned confessors and the like, but Teresa never ceased feeling that there was much danger, and much nonsense, in these mysteries, and in the *Vida* she ridicules those sisters who make raptures the sole object of their spiritual lives. 'They get it into their heads that it is *arrobamiento* (rapture). But I call it *abobamiento* (foolishness): for they are doing nothing but wasting their time and ruining their health.' So one must determine whether the body and soul have benefited afterwards. Like those induced by hysteria, or today by drugs, false visions leave the body feeling exhausted, or even wounded. But other genuine ones, once the initial fatigue has worn off and the coolness has passed, produce a very extraordinary invigoration. As with all deep experiences, not only the mystical kind, something valuable outlasts the event which is at times so strong that it changes one for the better, perhaps permanently, and in changing one may gain the capacity to alter his surroundings in entirely unexpected ways. Thus the supreme conclusion is a deeply joyous peace. The mystical event is transformed into practical expression at the moment Teresa, having 'seen' something marvellously noble and beautiful, feels the urgent necessity to have others share it with her.

Long after writing the *Vida* Teresa differentiates several mystical states, deriving the five main ones from the key concept of 'trance.' Many distinctions are drawn, such as that raptures seize one more suddenly than trances, that transports often develop into trances (which are deeper), that transports and spiritual wounds involve pain, but we begin to deduce the precise kind of mystical state the seraphic version is, without becoming entangled in these. Traditionally visions are divided into 'corporal,' 'imaginary,' and 'intellectual,' according to whether they communicate directly with the body, imagination, or intellect and spirit; the seraphic vision undoubtedly belongs to the 'intellectual' class. Because of Teresa's stress on total involvement, on the inseparability of the sensuous and spiritual, we may at first wonder how this could be. There is not only the testimony of her main prose works but her poem on God's dart of love which is no less sensuous than 'Let him kiss me with the kisses of his mouth' in her rendering of the *Song of Songs*. The same intensity comes out in many visions, such as the vision of Christ withdrawing with his right hand a large nail embedded in his left: 'He seemed to me to be tearing his flesh.' And in another vision, on a Palm Sunday, it appears that she could not receive the host because she felt Christ's blood overflowing her mouth and pouring down the front of her habit.

On such evidence as this, or on none at all, many have taken her character to be completely erotic and her spiritual passion to be sexual sublimation. Indeed she is erotic. The error is to limit that quality to the physical instead of realizing that God is the object of her love and her love is total and indivisible, including the body. In fact we should not wonder that this is an intellectual vision. Because intellectual visions are received completely passively they are the kind most likely to be genuine. They are also the highest kind of vision, and the easiest to recollect – a consideration which has a bearing on the clarity of Teresa's description. Above all, 'intellectual' does not directly contradict sensuousness as it may seem to. When Christ appeared to her it was 'always in his glorified flesh,' 'in his resurrected body.' The paramount feature of such visions is their total vividness, a vividness greater than anything seen by the physical eye. Divine communication is made directly with the intellect or spirit by means of 'spiritual feelings' (*sentimientos espirituales*), and these of course are not primarily sensory or emotional. What is perceived is analogous to sense perception, for the vision's entire sensory content comes from the intellect. However, in the total visionary experience all modes of perception are directly or indirectly involved, and the result is spiritual communication of the utmost kind. In this instance the abstraction we generally associate with intellect only intensifies the vividness. Teresa, who frequently found God's presence to be simultaneously vivid and abstract, would take this for granted. The two do not create a counter-tension but like pleasure and pain they ascend together and resolve into ecstatic bliss. To those in thrall to earthly experience alone, such an event is unthinkable.

> He presents Himself to the soul by a knowledge brighter than the sun. I do not mean that any sun is seen, or any brightness is perceived, but that there is a light which, though not seen, illumines the understanding so that the soul may have fruition. . . .[26]

Teresa's own description of the seraphic vision makes it clearer than the papal Bull of Canonization does, or Bernini and Crashaw do, that the vision appeared to her more than once in 1559 and after. She says it occurred 'sometimes' (*algunas veces*), though 'very rarely' (*por maravilla*). Teresa's is the one adequate account which survives from those we know to have experienced visionary wounds, among them St Gertrude, St

Agnes of Assisi, and Teresa's disciple St John, but the scene which has
been built up around the event comes in part from later cources.[27] One
evening Ana Gutiérrez, a sister in the convent of Ávila, heard cries and
groans coming from Teresa's cell and went to inquire. She found her
dishevelled and deeply agitated, her face all on fire. At first Teresa could
not speak. But as she recovered she said to the nun, 'Have I frightened you,
daughter? I wish you could have seen what I have seen.' The account
which follows is Teresa's in the *Vida*.

> It pleased the Lord that I should sometimes see the following
> vision. I would see beside me, on my left hand, an angel
> in bodily form – a type of vision which I am not in the
> habit of seeing, except very rarely. Though I often see
> representations of angels, my visions of them are of the type
> which I first mentioned [i.e. 'imaginary']. It pleased the
> Lord that I should see this angel in the following way. He
> was not tall, but short, and very beautiful, his face so aflame
> that he appeared to be one of the highest types of angel who
> seem to be all afire. They must be those who are called
> seraphim: they do not tell me their names but I am well
> aware that there is a great difference between certain angels
> and others, and between these and others still, of a kind that
> I could not possibly explain. In his hands I saw a long golden
> spear and at the end of the iron tip I seemed to see a point
> of fire. With this he seemed to pierce my heart several times so
> that it penetrated to my entrails. When he drew it out, I
> thought he was drawing them out with it and he left me
> completely afire with a great love for God. The pain was so
> sharp that it made me utter several moans; and so excessive
> was the sweetness caused me by this intense pain that one
> can never wish to lose it, nor will one's soul be content with
> anything less than God. It is not bodily pain, but spiritual,
> though the body has a share in it – indeed, a great share.
> So sweet are the colloquies of love which pass between the
> soul and God that if anyone thinks I am lying I beseech God,
> in His goodness, to give him the same experience.[28]

It is said that afterwards Teresa felt such discomfort from the heat that she asked Sister Ana to cut off her hair. When she did, it gave off such a wonderful scent that the nun wanted to keep it as a relic. Teresa immediately rebuked her: 'I order you not to think such nonsense and to throw that out with the trash!'

There was good reason for the reply. The inquisitional mood of Spain was dead-set against not only heretics but religious impostors. 'As there have been cases recently in which women have been subjected by the devil to serious illusions and deceptions, I began to be afraid. . . .'[29] Apparently she was referring to the scandals which had a little earlier shocked all Spain and sharpened the general spirit of scepticism and suspicion. Maria de la Visitación, a well-known prioress in Lisbon, had been exposed as a fake, and a Cordovan nun named Magdalena de la Cruz had confessed that her ecstasies were false and her miracles the devil's work. Many nuns of Teresa's own convent, the prioress included, questioned the genuineness of her visions, and some wanted to confine her in the convent prison-cell or expel her from the order. Her distinguished confessor Father Gaspar Diaz doubted the visions and refused to confess her. But there were also those whose doubts were overcome. A prominent noble of Ávila visited her to satisfy himself about her integrity. After gravely studying her face he spoke warningly to her: 'Do not forget Magdalena de la Cruz. Spain thought she was a saint and she was a slave of the devil.' Teresa murmured a painful reply: 'I never remember her without trembling.' That same noble later became one of her principal supporters. And eventually the seraphic vision, or visions were accepted as authentic.

If the fiery vision could not be summoned, at least Teresa was in a state of readiness. 'It is not we who put on the fuel; it seems rather as if the fire is already kindled and it is we who are suddenly thrown into it to be burned up.' The vital source of the seraphic vision here is also the conceptual principle of Crashaw's and Bernini's re-creations of the vision. Fire seems finally to prevail over water, though not to eliminate it: 'as water proceeds from the earth, there is no fear of its quenching fire, which is the love of God. The fire is absolute master and subject to nothing.' Like pleasure and pain, like abstraction and vividness, these opposing elements strengthen one another. Now there is the joy of 'seeing the vehemence of fire assuaged by water which makes it burn more.' In the realm of spirit, reversals of natural law have become familiar to us at least since the time when the celestial gravity in Dante began to pull upwards. Teresa shows the influence of heaven on earth by reversing nature here too – 'What a beautiful and wonderful thing it is that fire should cool water!'

The realization of harmony born out of earthly antipathies sometimes brings a burst of spiritual elation, as in *Way of Perfection.*

> Is it not a funny thing that a poor little nun of Saint Joseph's should attain mastery over the whole earth and all the elements? Fire and water obeyed Saint Martin; even birds and fishes were obedient to Saint Francis. . . . It was clear that they were masters over everything in the world, because they had striven so hard to despise it and subjected themselves to the Lord of the world with all their might. So, as I say, the water, which springs from the earth, has no power over this fire. . . .
>
> Water which comes down as rain from heaven will quench the flames even less, for in that case the fire and water are not contraries, but have the same origin.

The water of tears fans the flame; the fire which cools the water may freeze the worldly affections.

> Nothing worldly has warmth enough left in it to induce us to cling to it unless it is something which increases this fire, the nature of which is not to be easily satisfied, but, if possible, to enkindle the entire world.

Part II

Bernini's Teresan Cosmos

One

The Illusionistic Manner

Bernini's *Santa Teresa in Estasi* was first seen in 1651 when the Cornaro Chapel was opened. The statue by itself, without its setting, looked like a woman asleep with a sweetly smiling angel beside her. Or was she Cupid's victim resting in erotic languor? (PLATE II). On the whole the initial reactions were full of admiration,[30] though one tract of the times accused Bernini of pulling a pure virgin down to earth and making her into a prostrated, prostituted Venus.[31] Responses to the *Teresa* have been anything but temperate, and since baroque style has been more out of favour than in, the run of opinion has, through the centuries, been hostile or oddly off-centre. Two well-known French responses are those of le Président de Brosses who thought the work suggested a bedroom scene, and of Stendhal who rises to the pitch of 'Quel art divin! Quelle volupté!' The common charges of theatricality, sham piety, sentimentalism, sexual hyperbole, and vulgar taste are incompatible enough to reveal, as a rule, a certain impatience of understanding. It generally takes the form of the viewer passing too swiftly over the telling features of the statue, and of overlooking its chapel setting. Is Teresa quiet or excited? Erotic or ethereal? Though the word sounds censorious to many northern ears, the chapel is one of Bernini's most 'theatrical works, and one of his most elaborately illusionistic.

The marble-constant figure of Teresa after three centuries shows no signs of change, but conditions affecting how it is seen have changed radically. The Baroque has again come into its own. The quiescent interest in symbolic forms has been renewed along with the interest in organic structure. And illusionism, often regarded as no more than a superficial and tricky art of contriving appearances, is now understood to include deeper purposes. As in Bernini's work, it can now be seen as part of the symbolic process. Still more basically, the awareness of how we perceive works of art has increased greatly. The perfect perception of a work may be the ideal, but it is never attained. In practice we have almost ceased to accept the notion that perception can be total, perfect, and entirely objective. The way a painting or poem is perceived depends very much on the viewer's or reader's knowledge, memory, expectations, and personal predilections. The fact that nearly all works of art are symbolic makes it clear that the experience of each is to some degree fulfilled by us. What is actually presented, even in Elsheimer or van Eyck, is not completeness but the illusion of completeness.[32] What Bellini paints is not a whole landscape from nature but a planned landscape that has been validated by ocular experience and is ready for us to complete. A sonnet of Shakespeare is not a whole event but the symbolic structure for a whole event. From the point of view of artistic experience, it follows that even the most masterful illusion is successful to the extent that we assent to the illusion and participate in it.[33]

For Bernini artistic unity is a working assumption. Each undertaking was an instance of his unified view of life. In working out the subject of *Apollo and Daphne*, which he did in his twenties, he wanted to show the metamorphosis as a perfect fusing of hair and laurel leaves, body and tree trunk. Whatever the subject, he was at pains to make it reach a distinctive form of unity. As his biographer Baldinucci reports, Bernini rejected the legend (which the Renaissance revived from antiquity) that Zeuxis had made a Venus by combining the most beautiful parts of different women. The beautiful eyes of one could not be joined to the beautiful face of another.[34] It was in the unity of the parts that he found the greatest beauty.

As each word or image of a poem has a semantic environment, each visual element of a statue is part of the whole, is organically related to the total composition. St Teresa and the angel make a unified statue, but the statue is part of a larger conception. Bernini's total conception is the statue within the chapel. This is the full illusion – or almost the full illusion, since the chapel is also united to the church. As threads of meaning connect part to part we realize that perception of the Cornaro Chapel advances by an unpredictably associative process. Though the process differs with different arts, it applies to any work.

The temporal way in which poetical and musical compositions unfold for example, makes it obvious that the poet and composer exert more control over the sequence of perception than the visual artist does. The sculptor and painter, however, as artists for whom vision is primary, control perception in other ways. Crashaw can determine that one thing is to be known before or after another, and Bernini can show us in a flash that one thing is far more significant than another. Since no work of art is one pure sensation, this is only the beginning. From the first sensation others follow, some of them secondary and symbolic – Bernini's sculpture is also *seen tangibly* without being touched – and sensations set off not only new sensations but ideas, which in turn may lead reasonably to still other new sensations. Today it is becoming more common to assume that in art, as in everyday life, sensations and ideas constantly and naturally intermingle. It is separating them which is artificial and unnatural.

Therefore the perception of Bernini's *Teresa* and its chapel matrix is a mixed collection of responses, some fragmentary, some well formed, which by combining and re-combining sort themselves out until, at least for the time being, the viewer's experience of the work is completed. The process is particularly rich because in executing the chapel Bernini has brought several arts into play. We shall see that the poetry of Crashaw is served by the resources of other arts in a very different way. We may think that combining different artistic media is an invention of the seventeenth century. In fact the Parthenon was composed of architecture, sculpture, decoration, and probably painting. There, however, the individual arts are distinguishable, as they still are even in the early seventeenth century when El Greco built his remarkable chapel at Illescas. The quite rigid, Mannerist elements in the design of that chapel are harmonious but not tightly unified. In a number of Renaissance paintings architectural motives were made to harmonize with the architecture of their settings, but the decisive change comes when architecture and sculpture, or fresco and sculpture, are made entirely continuous, when the most multifarious and complicated works have a single dramatic impact. What sets this kind of baroque composition apart is not only the mass and variety of its elements but the way its diverse arts are *fused* into monomorphic unity. In Bernini's chapel, the earliest major example of such artistic fusion, distinctions of media all but melt away. By deliberate intention, only the sculpture is not directly and totally absorbed into the singleness of architecture, reliefs, painting, and decoration.

The illusion Bernini creates is unique and original. Bernini's figures are realistic yet idealistic, in feature and posture naturalistic looking and yet stylized and symbolically extended by other figures and forms. Some of these forms are from nature, some are imagined, but all of them by reflecting back on the central sculpture give it further meanings. The work is therefore out of reality and in reality, the clear intent being to join immediate reality (actuality) to the vaster Christian reality of heaven and earth.

Stylistically Bernini would not have made the separation between realistic and illusionistic strains in his works as later critics have. The illusionism serves the larger realism, the natural is comprehended by the supernatural. Although the phrase can refer to other, quite different styles like Leonardo's with its *sfumato* effects, 'naturalistic illusion' might seem adequate for Bernini, but 'naturalistic' now has the special colouring given it by nineteenth-century usage. For Bernini's style in general, 'realistic illusion' is preferable, as long as we take 'realistic' to signify the Christian cosmos of all that can be known, sensed, and intuited.[35] At best such broad, blunt terms only point in vague directions, yet the phrase combines the lifelike and metaphysical emphasis of his work.

Setting aside for the moment the symbolic meanings Bernini derives from abstract forms, the main tendency of the style is, in a hundred different ways, to make his figures and objects *look like life*. As Bernini says, 'art consists in everything being simulated although seeming to be real.'[36] Even in stage productions where he created fires, floods, and rising suns, he excluded from the stage real horses and other live animals. Those were ephemeral efforts, but the same principle operates in the Cornaro Chapel where Bernini alters and manipulates actuality so as to give his forms extra depth, beauty, and idea, as well as lifelikeness. A saint has a body, but the spirit and temperament must also come out and as they do the exterior form will invariably be affected. As Bernini said of his careful preparation for the bust of Louis XIV, the point was to arrive not at a synthesis of accurate views of him but at *le général de la personne*.[37] In carving a figure the artist's highest and most difficult aim – so goes an

11 St Teresa and the Seraph (S. Maria della Vittoria, Rome)

opinion which Bernini might have spoken but Leonardo actually wrote –
is to depict 'the intention of a man's soul,' to reveal through gestures and
movements of the limbs not only momentary states but a man's entire
inner life.

For the total impression of a work to be right Bernini performed endless
illusionistic tricks, most of them serious, some of them witty or playful.
Without interfering with serious intentions, he might also give a humorous
twist to a subject. The front views of the elephant in the obelisk statue
and the drinking lion of the Four Rivers fountain are joyously humorous,
and the busts of Thomas Baker and Paolo Giordano Orsini are ironic
conceptions. The cloak of Neptune curling into the form of a dolphin's
head is a witty comment, and the inscription below the elephant statue
is a broad pun. Water flowing in different shapes visibly joins a dolphin
and its pool, or helps support an obelisk. Or invisibly (as in this chapel)
natural light is let in from outside to illuminate indoor subjects. Many
times huge weights of marble are made to float lightly in the unity of
massive compositions. The first principle of his illusionistic technique
is to make marble resemble everything but marble – vegetation, animals,
angels, tapestry, wood, feathers, parchment, rising flames. But the main
object of all the technique, the grandest illusion, is to make marble have
the colour, resilience, and texture of flesh, for it is the human figure,
divinely created and divinely moved, which is the central motive of
Bernini's work (PLATE III).

Although his mythological subjects, his fountains, and many of his
portraits convey other kinds of meaning, nearly all his large masterpieces
are religious. The human figure is strongly Christian, as Bernini the man
was strongly Christian. Among the sins, he knew pride and avarice at
least, and his last years were darkly clouded by a sense of human weakness
and human inadequacy – the pain also of petitioning the Pope to suppress
the news of his brother's lawsuit.[37a] Yet he was an extremely devout man
whose life and attitudes generally upheld his faith. Though he had the gift
for success and knew how to avoid trouble, he was far more than a formal
Christian and recipient of papal commissions. He went to Il Gesù every
day for forty years, receiving Holy Communion many times a week, and
made a practice of annual retreats.

Consequently his art is peopled with angels, saints, and popes in a

III Aeneas, Anchises, and Ascanius, detail of Anchises' leg
(Galleria Borghese, Rome)

IV Gabriele Fonseca (S. Lorenzo in Lucina, Rome)

dazzling array of forms. A point for speculation is why Christ or Mary is never a major subject. In any case the figures Bernini carved from life, even early in his career and very markedly from the 1630's, express more individuality, animation, and naturalness of pose than had ever been seen in Rome.[38] The baroque penchant for spontaneity is as striking here as in the most dramatic examples of baroque literature and painting. Not all his figures, but a good number of them, including tomb figures, comprise a group of pieces that mark a new stage in European sculpture. The carving was revolutionary. Bernini shaped figures boldly and expressively, kneading vitality into them as God breathes life into substance (for he always imagined God to be in his hands as he worked). Baldinucci tells us that his greatest difficulty as a sculptor was in making the marble 'flexible' (*pieghevole*) but the difficulty is seldom if ever apparent.[39] On the contrary, busts like those of Scipio Borghese, Urban VIII, Montoya, and Fonseca seem to be entirely released from their marble confinement into a new spontaneousness of posture and expression (PLATE IV). Not posed like Roman senators or kings on thrones they are caught, as it were, in characteristic, natural moments, as though alive, breathing, and ready to turn and speak. This same fresh intensity and naturalness is also in several figures of saints. In this sense the figure of Teresa held completely in the grip of ecstasy is indeed 'theatrical,' for Bernini's intention is to present her, body and soul, with maximum intensity.

At the same time, the anti-literary emphasis in modern art may cause us to forget that Bernini was very distinctly a 'literary' artist. So, of course, were Rembrandt, Poussin, and Rubens. Bernini subscribed to the humanist view of art which accepted without question, but not without discrimination, the kinship shared by painting, sculpture, and poetry. More exactly, as Professor Wittkower has made pre-eminently clear, Bernini believed every work of art had to be informed by a *concetto* or literary theme.[40] Many contemporary artists made *concetto* signify an ingenious or clever kind of device or conception, sometimes in a sense close to that of poets of the time, an intricate or far-fetched metaphor, a likeness found in unlikeness — in short, they used it as an artifice more often than as a way of conceiving a work. But for Bernini, among others, the *concetto* served to centre the meaning of a subject, whether light or sublimely serious, and it was 'literary' in the sense that it can be formulated in words. His own observation that the colonnade at St Peter's reaches out like the motherly arms of the Church is his *concetto* for the colonnade. The tendency toward something of the kind was always there, in the early mythological subjects taken from writers like Virgil and Ovid, and in later scriptural subjects. For him imagination did not function abstractly or solipsistically but worked most fruitfully when it sought nurture and meaning in nature, whether in the forms of trees and animals, living people, pictures of people (he did the head of Charles I from Van Dyck's triple portrait), or literary and verbal presentations of realities he did not know at first hand. Perhaps he was farthest away from 'models' in producing full-length angels, Mary Magdalene, and the four Church Fathers, for in such cases he worked from tradition and his own imagination. The idea of *concetti* never hardened into dogma but remained useful to him in bringing subjects into final form. The Cornaro Chapel, far from being an exception, is a complex instance of their use.

The chapel was built in the seventeenth-century Roman church of S. Maria della Vittoria. As Baldinucci describes it, Bernini was the first to unite sculpture, architecture, and painting 'in such a manner that together they make a beautiful whole.'[41] The central group and the groups of four figures on each side are sculpture; the chapel's over-all design and the frame which holds saint and seraph are architecture; and the vault scene is primarily painting. Yet the plan includes more. Beyond these primary elements others strengthen the unity and increase the articulation: numerous relief figures, extensive marble-inlay work, and a profusion of decorative detailing. Exacting attention is given to every detail which could deepen, sharpen, or elevate the viewer's response. Besides the Carrara marble out of which the central figures and eight lesser figures are carved, the chapel uses about twenty other marbles, and in addition, stucco, fresco, bronze, gilt, and amber glass.

Out of this combination of techniques and materials Bernini fashioned a miniature cosmos on the four levels of death, earth, ecstasy, and eternity, with the brilliant sculpture of Teresa and the seraph placed at the centre[42] (PLATE V). That statue is now commonly regarded as the supreme example of Roman baroque sculpture, perhaps of all baroque sculpture, and the chapel as a whole may be the most daring example of illusionism in any Roman church.[43]

In church designs everywhere the arrangement of a heavenly vault above the earthly congregation is of course a ready consequence of the building's shape and function. Projections of a vertical scale of reality similar to Bernini's appear also in paintings, in the ascending levels of scores of Adorations, Assumptions, and Transfigurations, and in well-known works like Raphael's *Disputa* and El Greco's *Burial of Count Orgaz*. And, with significant variations which usually omit the explicit presentation of heaven, the same scale of reality appears in literature from before the time Shakespeare, Donne, Herbert, and Milton used it, until long after. That scheme known as the 'Great Chain of Being' defines a system of relationships extending from the foot of God's throne down to the smallest pebble on the shore, and since it was a well-known inheritance the expression of it is often implicit. Bernini's scheme and the 'Great Chain of Being' have in common the impulse to show within a restricted artistic design the subtle complications of man's place in the cosmos.

It was natural for Bernini to think in these transcendent terms, and frequently with forms more ample, grand, and free than any which preceded. Within little more than his lifetime, he and a few contemporaries notably Maderno, Borromini, Cortona, Rainaldi, and Fontana, substantially altered the appearance of Rome. The inward appearance of the city was also being changed not only by Bernini, Caravaggio, the Carracci, and Algardi, but by a whole flood of artists inspired by Counter Reformation sentiments. Bernini's own work may be seen fifty different places in Rome. In scale, extent, and variety its effect on Rome overshadows that of any other artist in a world capital. Even a sketchy impression of his work in and near St Peter's shows the breadth of his imagination. The comprehensive purpose of bringing the worshipper from the centre of Rome over the Tiber and along into St Peter's began (though the works themselves were not produced in this order) with the angels Bernini placed on both sides of Ponte S. Angelo.[44] After going from the river through the crowded Borgo one approached the broad piazza with its overwhelming view of the façade and dome of St Peter's. Four lines of lofty Doric columns forming wide arcs enclose most of the piazza space. Spread along the balustrades on top of the columns more than a hundred oversized statues of saints and martyrs loom like giant spectators above the piazza. In the centre of the portico, over the main entrance to the

v Cornaro Chapel, full view (S. Maria della Vittoria, Rome)

basilica, is Bernini's relief of the *Pasce Oves Meas,* and at the right end of it the large equestrian statue of Constantine which opens the way to his Scala Regia.

Within St Peter's the nave and side aisles are decorated by Bernini, often with symbolic emblems which simultaneously hide and reveal the mysteries of the faith. His great papal tombs and the opulent tabernacled altar of the Cappella del Sacramento are also important additions to the church, and well down the nave, at the crossing under Michelangelo's dome, rises his lofty, elegant, upward-swirling Baldacchino. Nearby, four elevated figures – his sixteen-foot statue of Longinus and three by other artists – are set into the piers he hollowed out for the four saints and their relics (PLATE VI). Finally the visitor arrives at the Cathedra Petri, the crucially important structure Bernini designed against the back wall of the church to contain the holy founder's chair. This unique edifice of architecture and sculpture completes the long perspective down the nave by rising lightly and magnificently from the floor up to a vision of the Holy Dove surrounded by angels in a sky of light (PLATES VII and VIII).

Those different works were executed under commissions from six popes, done step by step apparently without any master-plan or system of procedure.[45] The wonder is that Bernini could have produced so much coherence out of the divergent elements already present in the church. The full sweep of the work called on Bernini's skills as architect, sculptor, engineer, painter, and decorator, required the help of hundreds of artists and craftsmen, and went on for a period of fifty-six years – in contrast to the few workmen and seven years required for the Cornaro Chapel.

The chapel was built during the one period when Bernini was out of favour with the papacy and not involved at St Peter's. In that remarkable phase of his life he was at the peak of his powers, freshly inspired and highly inventive, as though responding to his own advice that 'those who do not sometimes go outside the rules never go beyond them.' He produced in that interval the Raggi tomb, the Raimondi Chapel, most of his best foundations, the statue of Truth, the late busts of Urban VIII, and the Cornaro Chapel. The chapel is minute next to the spectacle of St Peter's, but as an artistically unified work and a fully articulated picture

VI St Peter's, Baldacchino

VII St Peter's, nave view

of God's divine plan embracing the world's countless phenomena, it is Bernini's greatest triumph. Rather than being monumental and manifold, it is single, intense, and intimate in effect. If the vast spaces and riches of St Peter's fill one with the power and awe of the faith, the Cornaro Chapel expresses its mystery.

Bernini's capacity to participate in the lives of such saints as St Bibiana and St Longinus in the 1620's prepared him particularly well for the task of representing St Teresa. He seemed to realize that in this figure his visionary art reached its highest level of expression. As Baldinucci reports it, Bernini was in the habit of saying that the *Teresa* was the most beautiful work to come from his hand.[46]

Two

Approach to the Chapel

It was the Cardinal Federigo Cornaro who, in 1647 or soon before, engaged Bernini to build a family monument in S. Maria della Vittoria.[47] Carlo Maderno had built the church earlier in the century and in 1626 Soria finished it with a quite formal façade of the type at Il Gesù. That it was a Carmelite church may have influenced the decision to dedicate the chapel to St Teresa.

After 1622 when Teresa was canonized by Gregory XV (who a year earlier had knighted Bernini for the sculpture portraits done of him) her already considerable fame spread quickly through Mediterranean Europe and somewhat to the north. By the time Bernini started work on the Cornaro Chapel in 1645 he could have read the *Vida* in any of the ten Italian translations already available. It is probable that he did, even though extremely little is known about his reading. It seems reasonable to explain on other grounds the two or three small departures from the *Vida* which do occur.[48] What is impressive is the close likeness. Such details as the four episodes shown in the vault scene are not likely to have come from elsewhere, and the treatment of the saint herself is very close to what the *Vida* describes. It is extraordinary that the same conception of fire should also appear here, in the central statue and in other parts of the chapel. We might call fire Bernini's *concetto* for the work.

From the busyness of Via Venti Settembre one goes up a wide flight of stairs, though the small entrance in the compact façade, and forward through the church's sumptuously decorated nave to the chapel in the left transept. The scale of the church is relatively small – the whole of it would fit easily into one of the chapels off the transept of St Peter's – and the impression it makes is of privacy. All the chapels encroach on the aisle-less middle space with an enormous opulence of coloured marbles, gilt-work, sculpture, and paintings. The small amount of natural light gives the church a feeling which is internal as well as interior. The contrast is sharp between the noise and brightness outside and the heavy, glowing darkness of the interior. It is as if upon entering the church the visitor becomes physically and emotionally detached from active life before entering an area of rest and quiet. Then a second contrast occurs when the visitor passes through the church and comes up face to face with a supernatural event. The saint and seraph seem to belong to the same sphere of reality, but the reality is neither entirely earthly nor entirely mystical. A strangely indefinite aura surrounds the two figures. In a singular way which eludes photography the scene itself appears to change slightly as the viewer changes position or the light changes – a clear indication that the work is not made like a painting but is sculpture whose form and meaning vary according to one's angle of vision and to the quantity and kind of light it receives.

In designing and building the chapel there were problems to solve, and Bernini solved them with his usual skill. It has been suggested that he worked best when accommodating himself to difficulties – as in planning the Four Rivers fountains to relate to Sant' Agnese, in fitting S. Andrea al Quirinale on its plot by choosing an oval plan, in constructing a background for the Constantine statue in the portico of St Peter's, in designing the Scala Regia to overcome bad angles and cramped space. Had artists not often felt the challenge of external limitations, it is unlikely, for instance, that such a form as the sonnet would have had its long history. It is never apparent, at least, that Bernini was frustrated by limitations. One is struck rather by the spectacular freedom of many works. At S. Maria della Vittoria his chapel space was the next to last to be occupied. Here, as in St Peter's and elsewhere, his work required accommodation to circumstances. More than that, the space is unusually shallow and narrow in proportion to its great height (the dimensions being in a ratio of approximately 1 : 2 : 4). He made two main decisions: to build a kind of housing on the outside wall of the church, which deepens the space where Teresa is placed; and to organise the space on a strongly vertical axis.[49] While always keeping the saint and seraph prominent, in the rest of the chapel he piles layer upon layer, yet makes the layers interfuse in suggestive ways. At first the chapel seems to have the look

VIII St Peter's, Cathedra Petri

of dozens of other *seicento* chapels, a bewildering mottle of contrasting marbles in panels, pilasters, and borders. But as the viewer engages more fully with what is happening, the meanings on each level begin to stand out more clearly, both visually and symbolically. The eye very easily slides over the indistinct divisions and jumps the gap to the vault area, yet all the other zones become ultimately related to the luminous zone of Teresa.

It is interesting to see how Bernini uses motionless elements of architecture and sculpture to fill the chapel with motion. Like other artists of the time he had a vital interest in space. Sometimes he imagined it as something unearthly which has an independent existence of its own, a zone where mysterious events occur invisibly. Using Worringer's language one could say that Bernini sometimes interpreted space as metaphysical consciousness. As a rule it is complementary to matter, of course, but it can enclose specific meaning. The space surrounding his statue of David, for exzmple, is dramatic space which includes the viewer in David's action. Space also organizes movement. In the chapel this means *all* space, that which is open and that which is occupied, for no object, no area, seems to be completely at rest. Excepting the horizontal lines, everything is alive, vibrant, rising and flowing like a river of existence (PLATE IX). In addition to the motion in the marble patterns one notices the movement which light creates in the monochrome marble. When light strikes the highly polished areas it is diffused and deflected in various directions. Piaget and others have told us that we are born with a sense of movement, not statis, and that we know about space and objects in space only by learning about them. Originally then, the world looks to us like a continuous flow of organic evolution.[50] Unquestionably Bernini's intentions are well served by our natural and intuitive sense of movement – and some of his most 'sophisticated' illusionistic techniques are naturalistic. It is as if Bernini were inviting the viewer to subdue what is consciously known, namely the physical objects of vision, in order to draw up to the surface what is only subconsciously known, the movement. It may be that this is one of his illusionistic means for making objects into more than themselves. As in Teresa' writing, spiritual forms are being materialized at the same time physical forms are being spiritualized. The fluid representation of reality in the chapel bears directly on its total meaning. Bernini brings us to an experience which is distant, undivulged, and unusually deep – an experience which may give weight to Herbert Read's conviction that the specifically plastic or sculptural sensibility is more complex, and more uncommon in people, than the specifically visual sensibility.[51]

By placing the central figures high in the chapel and illusionistically deep in the architectural frame, Bernini is exerting considerable control over our vision. As a rule he intended each work to be seen from an optimal vantage point, as many sculptors had in the previous generation. Figures like St Bibiana and St Longinus are recessed in niches which shield them from their surroundings and set some limits on the viewer's position. Later on, the Daniel and Habakkuk, among other figures, come so close to bursting out of confinement that their niches only very slightly define the viewer's approach. In the period between, the Cornaro Chapel expresses this idea of confinement in its extremest form. Bernini prevents us from letting the eye play freely over the figures from very oblique angles. He wants a frontal view which is determined not merely by the columns and pilasters at the sides of the architectural frame but by the fullest possible view of the two facing figures. That describes a narrow line of optimal vision running from near the altar rail out beyond the middle of the nave. If one may speak of an optimal *point* it would be on that line, not close enough to hide Teresa's right hand or any of her face, yet not distant enough to lose a view of the statue which is quite steeply upward. The importance of that angle of vision is made clear in Bernini's preliminary drawing of Teresa's head and face as seen from below.[52] A position far back from the chapel would also be liturgically inappropriate, and in addition would interfere with the sculptural clarity of the figures. Indeed it is difficult from any place in the church to see the whole chapel in one view. The shallowness and height may be another instance of Bernini making a virtue of necessity. It serves his inward-looking purpose to have the viewer see less than the total chapel at once. Only by directing his eye from part to part can he possess the whole, and the parts can be easily brought into union only by the mind's eye.

The control Bernini exerts over our vision has contradictory results. By presenting Teresa enframed, illuminated, and fully visible he invites the viewer's participation in the event. Vision can flow freely from the viewer's eyes to the sculptured figures. On the other hand, by setting

Teresa deep, enclosing her in the frame, and raising her above eye-level, Bernini holds the viewer off. Since the eye is on a level just above the altar top it seems almost as if one perceives her only by passing over the horizontal barriers of altar top, candle ledge, and base of frame.

The ambiguity involved in reaching Teresa only heightens the importance of the mystical event being presented. The baroque interest in climax comes into early works like the *David* and the *Apollo and Daphne*, where the climaxes are self-contained; it continues to appear later, but in new forms. In depictions of saints, pre-eminently Teresa and Constantine, the idea of climax is developed metaphysically. The temporal, emotional, dramatic reality of Teresa's ecstasy holds steady for our view, but the transcendent spirituality of the event alters what we see. The sense of this being an earthly or theatrical scene partially fades out. What appears as a physical event in space is also an event of indefinitely long duration. The statue depicts an experience in which space and time are indistinguishable. Bernini is concerned that the viewer possess more of the event than can be seen. Teresa's climax as seen from a restrictively human point of view belongs to the moment, but as seen from the divine point of view which we imagine, it is timeless and endless. Continuity and climax cease to be contradictory. One is allowed to engage in the experience as both a sublime human moment and a divine event which has taken on qualities of the eternal.

Since the ecstasy represented in the chapel is a rare event among human beings, Bernini does not make it accessible to easy or indifferent approach. As we walk toward a painting on a wall, says one art critic, at a certain point it ceases to be a painting. The artistic illusion is suddenly shattered and we see only paint dabs of different shapes and colours. In roughly the same way, a marble form when seen at too close range will lose its wholeness. Here that does not happen. Bernini creates an illusion which is a mystery, and he is careful to make the illusion impossible to destroy.

Three

The Enlarging Cosmos

According to an old saying of the mystics, the soul holds the Divine Word as a shell holds the ocean. Art also knows something about the contravention of physical laws. In the chapel the spectator's eye can ultimately enclose the cosmos. Sooner or later attention will come to rest on the pavement, the zone of mortal death. Two half-length figures of death appear there, bone-white skeletons circled in darkness (PLATE X). Around them marbles of contrasting shades, a balck plaque, low-toned wall panels and door frames, give an effect of relative dimness. The two marble tarsia figures gesticulate energetically, one looking oddly like a dramatic singer, the other like an orchestra conductor. They contribute to the 'theatrical' atmosphere which Bernini is developing in the chapel, but this is not the meaning. Apparently they are expressing stark wonder at the ecstasy being shown above them. Since they must be related to the Cornaro family in the sepulchre beneath the pavement, they may also be begging for God's mercy in attitudes of anguish. These death figures, flat though they are, have no less animation than the skeletons on Bernini's papal tombs at St Peter's. If death shall rise it shall rise in the urgent energy of these figures.

On the second level immediately above the darkened zone of death a strange little drama is being enacted on the side walls. This is the viewer's own zone, the heterogeneous world where he is conscious of daily reality and possibly of more. It includes the people in the very fine bronze relief of the Last Supper on the altar face and those somewhat higher up in the recessed frames on the side walls (PLATE XI). Through the dimness which enfolds everything in the chapel except Teresa and the seraph, one discerns that the marbles of this area have more colour than those below – the greens, ambers, and golds suggestive of natural growth,

ix Cornaro Chapel, central section

x Cornaro Chapel, pavement from above

xi Cornaro Chapel, altar relief

the pinks and reds suggestive of clay, even of flesh and blood. If the colours and an aggregate of twenty-one human forms imply anything about this zone it is man and the earth (Frontispiece).

The high-relief altar front – which Bernini may or may not have designed – is a dramatization of the Last Supper. As a subject for the Communion table its significance is obvious, but its special appropriateness in this chapel should not be overlooked. The primary action in this zone, however, takes place in the frames on either side. Each frame holds four men, all of them posed informally, slightly theatrically, and their attention goes in various directions (PLATE XII). They belong to the devout and distinguished Venetian family of Cornaro, some of whom are recalled in paintings by Titian, Tintoretto, El Greco, Veronese, and Gentile Bellini. Seven of the eight Cornaros shown here were cardinals, and all but Federigo, who ordered the chapel, lived in sixteenth-century Venice.

As we see these figures they are talking, meditating, reading Scripture, and staring into space. That their attention is dispersed and their positions somewhat random are two reasons they have so often been compared to spectators in theatre boxes. In fact they are kneeling or sitting behind draped prie-dieus, against backgrounds of church architecture (PLATE XIII). The treatment of the figures is extraordinarily spontaneous and lifelike. Only two of them are drawn with individual personalities, the rather hard-faced Doge tucked away at the far end of the left frame, and his son the Cardinal Federigo, who is seen looking out of the right frame[53] (PLATE XIV). This latter, the most fully developed portrait, has the look of a shrewd and urbane aristocrat, and the two together effectively enlarge the range of human meaning in this zone. Considering their relative smallness in the chapel design, one is impressed by the care given to these figures and their settings, a care which is not gratuitous, we may be sure, in a composition where each element is part of a pattern.

Why do they face in different directions, and what kind of meaning is in the illusionistic church settings behind them? The architectural features, barrel-vaulting, fan-top niches, the square coffers with rosettes, and so forth, are more or less Renaissance, but the settings are wrenched far out of perspective and look only half real. The *trompe l'œil* of the backgrounds extends the spectator's view outwards in both directions,

XII Cornaro Chapel, right perspective frame

XIII Cornaro Chapel, left perspective frame, close-up

as though the chapel's actual architecture, in particular the aedicule holding Teresa, is reaching out into the frames at each side. The coffering which lines the top inside of Teresa's oval frame is picked up again in the illusionistic church settings. The effect is again of depth – depth in both space and time. As can happen, the spatial distinctions carry temporal connotations, and the two coincide or even merge. In both frames, from the projecting fronts of the prie-dieus to the far corners of the church backgrounds, space recedes through several gradations. The figures themselves lie at different degrees of depth (PLATES XIII and XV). Recession in time and recession in space go hand in hand: the architecture refers back to the previous century when seven of the Cornaros were alive, and the association is easily made between that point in time and the historical Teresa's point in time. But since the primary drift of meaning is in the opposite direction, toward the future and transcendental, it may be more appropriate to say that the ecstatic event which took place in historical time comes through from the Cornaros to the living Cardinal Federigo and hence to Bernini's synchronous re-enactment of it.

By placing the Cornaros above the viewer's level and almost on a level with the saint, Bernini makes us aware of them as human intermediaries between us and her. The living world they occupy is the same world in which the viewer stands, and their living attitudes make them part of the present as well as the past.[54]

The temporal bonds which serve to join together different areas of the chapel also bind the viewer into the complex. Lively as the figures are, they appear to symbolize humanity which must die, but humanity which dies into the future life afforded by faith. Yet faith makes no promises, and so, contradictorily, their white-marble appearance, always less light than Teresa's, partially attaches them to the progress of life expressed by the chapel's scheme of polychromes.

Common as polychrome sculpture was in Spain, in Hispanic Naples, and subsequently in the German north, Bernini, though an artist in polychromy, did not choose to make any of his important figures in anything but white marble (excluding, of course, a number of bronze figures). The naturalistic intent of polychrome figures sometimes went the whole way – glass eyes, actual fabric for garments, human hair and eyelashes. To Bernini such practices were as ludicrous and erroneous as

XIV Cornaro Chapel, figure of Federigo Cornaro in right perspective frame

xv Cornaro Chapel, two figures in right perspective frame

live horses on the stage. It was a matter of letting the waters of art overflow the real shore. He believed instead that monochrome figures, if properly modelled and dhown in the right light, were *more* lifelike in that they could open up dimensions of character which literalistic figures keep closed.

But polychrome figures are a different thing from polychrome settings. The latter are a true mark of his style, as in the celebrated settings for Urban VIII and Alexander VII in the tombs at St Peter's. Indeed he used coloured marbles for nearly everything *but* his figures. Of the churches he designed, S. Andrea al Quirinale, which pleased him most, has been well-known for its dramatic lighting, oval plan, and exuberantly buoyant cupola, but it is the arrangement of the red-mottle Sicilian jasper which gives the church its magnificent unity (PLATES XVI and XVII). The treatment of the marbles in the Cornaro Chapel was equally sensitive and painstaking. One of Bernini's best critics calls the chapel the most perfect example of complex colour relationships he ever produced.[44] Though the twenty-odd marbles are not particularly rare they are extremely rich and various, and virtually all, excepting those of the side walls and other less conspicuous areas, are ancient. The marbles used in most *seicento* churches of Rome were usually appropriated from villas, tombs, and other ready sources, many of them originally Greek, in this case the green of the pilasters (*verde antico*) from Thessaly, the reddish black of the columns (*africano*, meaing simply dark) from Teos, and others from Cios and Skyros (and still others came from Egypt, Africa, Spain, France, Belgium, and Turkey).[44] As far as possible, refinements of colour, veining, clouding, and direction of grain were taken into account. But, as the sources of ancient marble gradually dwindled it became more and more common to face surfaces with pieces of marble ingeniously joined together, sometimes, as here, by using a dozen or sixteen pieces for one panel, and even more for the pilaster faces. Strong contrasts of borders against panels and light tones against dark give the marbles a feeling of great vividness and vibrancy, in comparison, for instance, to the very similar chapel opposite. A tremendous amount of energy is generated, above all by the large flowing patterns of the onyx panels beside and below St Teresa. The decorative element is always present of course, but so are symbolic motives. While no panel, column, or pilaster 'says' anything, several broad effects add to the meaning, according to Bernini's 'literary' mode of composing. Colour is more than the earthly, human colours already mentioned. On Teresa's level there are remarkable sea-greens and wavy browns which surround her almost white figure like a world. As difference implies likeness, some connection must reveal itself in the contrast between her quite pure tone and the natural colours beside her. Involved with colour yet also independent of it is the comprehensive effect of the tones: it appears, though ever so lightly, that ascent of spirit is expressed by the tones gradually becoming lighter in the chapel from the floor up to the vault[57] (PLATE XVIII). From the start, the murky light of the chapel did not sharpen the effect, and by now the grime from candle-smoke and city dust has made it still dimmer. Such regular gradations as can be observed are essentially those between the large areas of dark or black marble in the pavement and the richer colours above. They are not strong, clear, and regular, however, for that would seriously interfere with the fluency of the design. All elements of the chapel are kept actively related to Teresa. Or, it is as true to say, her luminous presence radiates everywhere, spreading through the lower chapel and into the vault.

The active, airy, light-filled area which is the vault of heaven is executed with unusual illusionistic tact, according to Bernini's design but by the hand of his most able assistant, Guidobaldo Abbatini. The artifice is the conversion of a narrow area (the depth of the entire heavenly scene is some ten feet) into a full-blown celestial skyscape of clouds, angels, and wings all swirling freely toward the Holy Dove at the top (PLATE XIX). On their larger scales the Cathedra Petri at St Peter's and the wide-realmed heavens of Pozzo, Cortona, and Gaulli give the same sense of endless spiritual ascent. The dove in the circle of celestial light is the Holy Spirit and in addition, as a symbol for the inspired knowledge of divinity, the dove is specifically associated with Teresa. In the latter sense we imagine Teresa and the dove in a union which is not about to take place but has already occurred.

On the front arch of the vault other angels fly, twist, and play, drifting toward the peak where larger angels hold the wreath and inscription which celebrate Teresa's glorification. The free-form, illusionistic mass clinging to the upper walls of the vault and entirely covering its top surface is more than a gilded stucco vision of heaven. It is Teresa's

XVI S. Andrea al Quirinale, main altar (Rome)

XVII S. Andrea al Quirinale, section of cupola

apotheosis. Some measure of the integral importance of this heavenly scene in the total design can be taken if one recalls that, with just one or two exceptions, the major architects of the period – Bernini, Borromini, Cortona, and Rainaldi – allowed no space in their churches for grand ceiling paintings.[58]

The dominant representation of her in the architectural frame below reappears above in a variety of after-forms. A full-length likeness of her, added later, stands out quite strongly against the vault window. But even without that image the same point is made by the four subdued scenes painted on the vault walls which recall events from before and below (PLATE XX). The consummation is interpreted in the same way by both Crashaw and Bernini: Teresa in glory is Teresa risen out of the scenes of her life. Her spiritual translation somewhat resembles that of S. Andrea in Bernini's church. Both are shown in life first, and then in after-life, one in an altar painting, the other in marble, but where S. Andrea is surging up and breaking through the pediment over the altar, Teresa has already reached her heavenly goal (PLATE XVI).

Some kind of dramatic action is taking place on every level, from the animated skeletons in the death-pavement to the life-scenes in the empyrean. Nothing moves, yet everywhere there is movement, in the multiple actions and, more abstractly, in the flowing marble patterns and the upthrusting lines of the architecture. The top zone is cut off from those below by the horizontal lines of the friezes, borders, and jutting string-course (PLATE V). Because its pale colours and dull gold areas moderate the brilliance of the vault it does not compete with the bright figure of Teresa below but completes the meaning of her ecstatic moment by projecting it distantly upwards through time and space. The buoyant, billowy scene, usually not strongly lighted by daylight from the window, appears to gather its light from the white field surrounding the Holy Dove. From the earthly point of view its lesser brightness also keeps the sight of heaven distant.

Down lower, the Cornaro figures in their settings live, so to speak, in the reflected light of the central statue. Very deliberately Bernini has placed the two groups in positions from which it is impossible to see St Teresa. Of the eight, only one is facing her directly, and because the frame around her blocks his vision, he is unable to see her (PLATE XIII).

XVIII Cornaro Chapel, lower half

Although the Cornaro family members either cannot or will not *see* the ecstasy being enacted there, they must have some connection with it. Considering their placement in the chapel, the ecstasy is their *raison d'être*. Yet even though we might expect Bernini to show them as spectators, he chooses not to. They are in the human condition, but, as their high position on the wall emphasizes, they are above and beyond the ordinary viewer. If they do not possess the ecstasy visually, we may imagine that they participate in it by some other means.

As other parts of the chapel remind us, a saint's vision belongs partly to an order of experience which transcends mind and senses. The circumstances suggest that since one cannot gain access to the mystery by direct means, then indirect and symbolic means may succeed. The Cornaros are concerned with the mystery, but they do not see it. At this point it would appear that Bernini is transforming sight into insight, and using the figures to invite deeper penetration into religious ecstasy.

The repute of Bernini's Teresa, the extravagance of showing the private condition of the saint '*in pieno abbandono*' (the phrase of Muñoz) and wide open to public view, may not immediately persuade one that Bernini's treatment was orthodox. But it was in every respect orthodox and acceptable. After several decades the restraints placed on art by the Council of Trent were not administered so strenuously. Since the realistic treatment of devout subjects was condoned and even encouraged, Bernini could not have feared official criticism. All around him the suffering flesh of saints and martyrs was visible as never before. In Possevino's pronouncement, if an artist's work genuinely demands it, Christ himself can be shown 'afflicted, bleeding, spat upon, with his skin torn, wounded, deformed, pale, and unsightly.'

In art Bernini, like most men of genius, was both innovator and traditionalist, but in religion he was pure traditionalist. Teresa is the product of his total Christianity. As a Christian he saw nothing in isolation, everything joined to everything, if not visibly and overtly, then invisibly, internally. The heavenly and the earthly, objects, ideas, individuals, modes of movement and of time all aspire to unity and arrive there. The manner of many Bernini figures implies many connections with others. Montoya, Costanza Buonarelli, Urban VIII, Louis XIV, all communicate with other people or with God, as if their existences depend

XIX Cornaro Chapel, vault view from below

on it. In the chapel the unseeing witnesses to the ecstasy are dependent upon Teresa, while she, in a state of enthralment, has passed beyond her conscious dependence on God and on people into transcendence.

The numerous references and cross-references to time and place in the chapel point to a single, simple truth about mystical experience: it cannot be constrained by the grip of time and place. If time points back from the moment Bernini was building the chapel, it also points forward from that moment, by virtue of the chapel's continuing existence. The mysterious event first occurring in 1559 is also occurring in 1650. Nor does it cease at the moment the chapel is finished, for it occurs again as often as new spectators are there to experience it.

Four

Saint and Seraph

The figure peering from the right side is trying in vain to see the radiant saint and seraph in the centre. Their dominance in the chapel results in part from the special way they are lighted. At the top of the housing Bernini ordered to be built on the church's outside wall are several windows which let in light from the outside, after which it is filtered by a pane of amber glass to soften its effect on the stark whiteness of the marble figures as it falls on them from above (PLATE IX). Bernini's innovation of bringing natural light in from outside, which he had used earlier, comes into several other works, to particularly good effect behind the Cathedra Petri and over the reclining figure of the Blessed Lodovica Albertoni. The tinted light makes the 'flesh' of Teresa and the seraph look more real, yet also slightly transparent and impalpable. The light was originally gentler and less white than the light which now pours down from fluorescent tubes concealed in the architectural frame. A strange paradox when natural light is preferable to artificial in creating the illusion of a mystical event! However, if the imaginative effort is made to recover the miraculous scene as Bernini created it, one must take into account those things which interfere with both the mystery and the realism of the work. Nearly all photographs belie the subject by lighting it strongly from the front and by recording it horizontally rather than from the viewer's lower angle of vision. Light, we quickly discover, is a crucial element of the form, and since it has symbolic value, of the meaning too. The effluence of God issuing from a divine, unseen source above, comes down the golden shafts behind Teresa to bathe her in heavenly brightness (PLATE XXI).

Like movement, light is a crucial artistic principle with which baroque artists experimented extensively, and often mastered for their individual

xx Cornaro Chapel, right section of vault

purposes. Whether one thinks of Rodin, Michelangelo, or Bernini, sculptors and architects in general use light for much more than the ordinary necessities of vision. For the painter it is something different. Relatively speaking, the light in a painting is intrinsic, inherent, because it is *painted in*. In celebrated instances like Caravaggio's *Vocation of St Matthew*, Rembrandt's *Christ before Pilate*, or la Tour's *St Sebastian and St Irene*, intrinsic light composes the painting and produces the drama. On the other hand a sculptor understands that light is absolutely essential – precisely the right light, in tone, in amount, in angle or angles – if a work is to achieve realization. It is relevant to the Teresan statue that when light strikes mat surfaces it is sopped up, and when it strikes polished surfaces it is fractured and flung off into dark areas. Consequently the light which accentuates details can also blur them and alter the total form. Yet that very blurring can also unite the form. Appropriate lighting can give to a work a feeling of unreality, or heightened reality, while preserving its realism.[59] Here, by a kind of magic, light causes the shadows, dull areas, and bright points to coalesce. It serves the purpose of unity, which in this case is indistinguishably artistic and spiritual. A single form combining the two figures is dimly visible, although parts of it dissolve and escape into the light. Light determines the comparative significance of different areas of the chapel, and in a symbolic sense attaches Teresa to divinity.

The figures of the saint and seraph, which are Bernini's own, are done with evident care and devotion. Excepting the slight possibility that he carved 'the last Cardinal Cornaro' (as Baldinucci says), it is only certain that Bernini did the central group, although of course he designed the chapel as a whole and supervised the work. In a zone beside and above the terrestrial zone Teresa appears life-size and expressively lifelike, and beside her appears grace in the form of an angel. To be sure, the life-likeness is illusionistically expanded to the breaking point. The saint's facial features are classically idealized, seemingly perfect and imperishable (PLATE XXII) – she is the true sister of the Apollo Belvedere and Bernini's own Apollo – and the body beneath the folds of her habit is unnaturally long, the drooping hand and extended foot drawn out into a Mannerist look (PLATE IX). In her figure Bernini continues to maintain his style of realistic illusion. At the same time, the carving of individual features

xxi St Teresa and the Seraph, view from eye level without frontal illumination

xxii St Teresa, side view of head

such as the mouth, fingers, and toes is also relatively true to life. But the secret of the sculpture is that Teresa is quite withdrawn and nothing like as fully revealed as she at first appears to be.

The large frame around Teresa and the seraph floats them in space so that they seem to have lost contact with the surrounding world. Below them the only support is a shadowy cloud. Behind them a panel of alabaster suggests indefinite and tenebrous distance. The long metal shafts of golden light which partly obscure the panel only augment the effect of her isolation from the world. Intentionally or not, Bernini's arrangement expresses in graphic terms the distress of losing human connections felt by the historical Teresa in advanced states of contemplation. Though accessible to our perception, this marble Teresa does not perceive us.

In contrast to her white-monochrome intensity the frame is a mottle of colours. Beside her silence and secrecy the patterns of onyx move unquietly, spreading out toward other shapes and shades of marble in that part of the chapel. In good light one sees that the most vivid colouring in her vicinity is the green (*verde antico*) of the pilaster faces, which deepens into darker green next to the alabaster panel (FRONTISPIECE). Especially at close range the colour and pattern of these greens have a marine effect, as though bright flecks of foam and sunlight were disturbing the water. The effect is more natural and literal than symbolic. The earth colours all around, particularly the rich brown of the panel behind, complete the impression of a terraqueous world. All these life-infused colours, together with the death colours below, appear to converge on Teresa, as though impinging on her from earthly life and rising up to her from the sea depths. Their meanings unite in her just as prismatic colours all unite into white. Teresa's light is not all her own, however. As she says, in what only seems to be a paradox, visionary light 'is like natural light and all other kinds of light seem artificial.' From the spectator's point of view the pavement of the chapel is passing death, the celestial landscape an anticipation, and the greens of nature a principle of ever-reviving life.

The distance and isolation which seal in the meaning of ecstasy begin slowly to reveal it. Having been held at a respectful distance, the viewer is ultimately summoned forward by the sprung shape of the architectural aedicule (PLATES V and IX). Seen thus, the frame resembles a richly classicized bow-front proscenium with a small opening. It is as if Bernini had begun with a heavy, flat frame whose pediment and entablature rest solidly on its double columns and pilasters, and then by main force had bent the entire frame into an advancing curve, breaking the pediment and entablature, in order to reveal the scene within.

The face of the Correggiesque angel is openly communicative. He (if angels have gender) has descended on the shafts of light and is poised with the dart of love in his hand (PLATE II). The softened lines of his body and arms bear no resemblance to those of the armed soldier or hunter. His left leg puts him in a position completely unsuited to an aggressive act. Instead he is an idealized picture of grace and celestial gentleness, a member of the benign order of the universe and Christ's agent of love. His serenity stands out against the busier, more existential appearance of most of the Cornaros. The face is flawlessly sweet and luminous, not ruddy like those of other seraphs but glowing with cool, white ardour [60] (PLATE XXIII). And his face is silently fixed on Teresa.

All lines of perception meet in her. The death-figures, the witnesses, and the glorification to come, compose the Teresan cosmos. Heaven and earth commune in her figure, its light radiating over the forms and into the space of the vertical chapel. The frame encloses her as she in turn encloses the mystery. On the earthly level where visitors come to worship, the relief of the Last Supper makes clear the sacramental purpose Bernini has in mind. Though common enough as a subject on earlier altar faces, it is noticeably absent on those in Roman baroque churches.[61] Nearly always it is decorative marbles which appear there, not narrative scenes. In this chapel the Last Supper relief serves as the liturgical equivalent to Teresa's more intense and exceptional communion with God.

The ecstasy itself is expressed solely in her figure, in the details and suggestions of her form and features. The 'plastic sensibility' which Bernini calls upon is responsive to volume, among other things, and in this instance the volume contains meaning. The outer form refers inwardly. It has an existence of its own, yet it exists also for what it discloses beneath the surfaces of her skin and clothing – provided, of course, that it makes sense to speak of outer and inner form separately, as Bernini would not. But the figure does not reveal itself quickly.

When did the ecstasy occur? How did it occur, and what is the seraph's part in it? Teresa's face and posture seem to show her still engaged in

XXIII The Seraph, view of head

XXIV St Teresa, front view of head

the ecstasy, or just released from it. But since the seraph is holding the dart as if ready to plunge it into her, perhaps the event has not yet occurred. His somewhat relaxed posture only complicates the question. And again, if the dart has already been thrust into her breast, no wounds are evident. Finally we cannot say whether the event is to come, is occurring, or has come and gone.

Bernini presents Teresa in the simplest terms possible, without cross, beads, cincture, or sandals. Choosing to interpret the word *descalzo* literally, he omits her rope sandals. It is an essential Teresa he creates, a woman of indeterminate age – is she twenty or fifty? – whom he clothes in a plain, voluminous habit which makes her body all but disappear. Her reposeful and rapturous face (which a lesser artist might make into a monochrome mask) is carved into animation. The naturalistic appearance of the eyes Bernini achieved by incising very deeply beneath the lids, and by chiselling out the space around them to produce the bluish impression he saw in the faces of living people (PLATE XXIV). The face is idealized yet strongly sensuous. Of the erotic quality so often commented on, fleeting signs are visible in the hands and feet, in the contours of the mouth, chin, and brow, and in the posing of the body beneath the robes (PLATE II). Unquestionably the figure of Teresa is erotic, but in no exclusively physical sense. The facial expression is full of passion yet its spiritual content distinguishes it very readily from, for instance, the pure earthly passion showing in the face of Costanza Buonarelli. Teresa seems to be breathing, her mouth warm, moist, and a little opened as if releasing the silent moan mentioned in the *Vida*: '. . . not aloud, for that is impossible, but inwardly, out of pain.' Without the overwhelming spiritual motive, Teresa would indeed be the woman William James saw as carrying on 'an endless amatory flirtation' with God.[62] The motive is not overlooked by Simone de Beauvoir in explaining the body's role in ecstasy – the same role it has had in Christian ecstasy generally, one might add, for not until recent centuries has it been necessary to explain that in genuine religious ecstasy body, mind, and spirit are all involved. As she says, St Teresa 'in a single process seeks to be united with God and lives out this union in her body.'[63] But we recall that Teresa herself speaks at first-hand about this aspect of ecstasy: 'it is not bodily pain, but spiritual, though the body has a share in it – indeed, a great share (. . . *no deja de participar el cuerpo algo, y aun harto*).' In union Teresa's human and divine natures both belong to God. Teresa's moment of ecstasy looks to the resurrection of body and spirit alike.

Yet the moment is obscure. As in the *Vida*, Teresa's eyes are closed. She does not see the seraph of her vision with her physical eyes. Though he is necessarily visible to our wakened sight, he is visible only to her internal sight. Bernini seems almost to be asking that the seraphic vision be 'seen' through the saint, that it be re-experienced imaginatively through what is taking place within Teresa's visible form. What shows is a symbolic presentment of her inward state. Enigmatic as that may be, we look more closely still.

In Teresa's hands and feet her simultaneous excitement and quiescence are revealed (PLATE II). The right hand resting relaxed in her lap and the left hanging limply at her side make known the body's assent to transport, and the exhaustion which follows. But her feet express a tenseness. The foot held perpendicular to the extended leg is flexed as though in spasm, and her taut right foot, almost invisible in the filmy billow of cloud, presses against it so hard that the cloud seems to resist like stone (PLATE XXV). The somewhat regular folds of her rumpled habit apparently result from her inner vibrancy, from the agitation and strong fibrillations of her body in the grip of transport. To judge from the contours of the habit – and we should be able to, since Bernini's handling of drapery became more abstract and symbolic as time went on – the tautness and vibrancy may run through Teresa's whole body. But does it? The slim, indistinct form under the robes appears to be fully relaxed also. Perhaps the tension is only in the lower parts of the body and the rapture at this precise moment has released its grip on her upper body and is working its way out through her lower extremities.

The figure of Teresa is a perfect mingling of tension and relaxation. But ordinary logical structures collapse before the spiritual reality. The carefully wrought ambiguities point to the ecstasy without encompassing it. Something is inevitably missing. The limits of understanding have been reached and we, like Dante's pilgrim or Milton's Adam – or Bernini – are not privileged to go further.

Yet we are sure that there is an ecstasy, and that ecstasy, as Bernini and St Teresa show it, and Crashaw shall, is a condition transcending

xxv St Teresa, view of feet

the ordinary opposites of pleasure and pain, body and spirit, motion and rest, weight and weightlessness, time and timelessness. Bernini gives us the figure of a woman uniquely posed, neither sitting nor lying down. The tendency for the weight of her body to make her fall is weaker than the tendency for her cloud-borne figure to rise. The highest folds of her habit are more buoyant than air. The ecstasy is a troubled state of transition between existence on earth and existence above. While her exterior nature occupies space and time, very little of her interior nature, the secret scene of her experience, is still in the world.

The actual saint returned from her visionary moments to live her daily life, the same woman yet spiritually heightened and invigorated. Gradually these moments led to permanent change. She speaks of being touched by a kind of dreaminess. God, she explains, 'has given me a life which is a kind of sleep; when I see things, I seem nearly always to be dreaming them.'[64] The borderline between actuality and spiritual transcendence is obliterated by Bernini and St Teresa both. Though Bernini's marble likeness remains fixed it always seems ready to rise into the celestial zone. Teresa's life in the statue, and in history, has by now become more than earthly. Her resemblance to sleep may actually be her awakening from time. As surely as Teresa's ecstasy is happening within time, it is also happening beyond time, and we are beholding an event which has no duration.

Five

The Movement of Marble

The ceiling Gaulli painted at Il Gesù is Bernini's idea of what monumental painting should be: a massive and multifarious scene worked out into coherence by a combination of media. One of the celebrated pieces of late baroque Rome, this spreading spectacle of men, angels, smoky clouds, and empyreal light spills out over the architecture on every side. In a generalized way it exemplifies what Gaulli said was the most valuable maxim learned under Bernini's long tutelage, that every rendering of the human figure should, if possible, express movement.[65] Movement is virtually a first principle of Baroque style. Yet it is hardly the exclusive possession of any one style. In Focillon's opinion all works of art in all media are 'motionless only in appearance.' Movement, he goes on, 'seems to be set fast – arrested, as are the moments of time gone by. But in reality it is born of change, and it leads on to other changes. . . .'[66] Bernini began very early to express movement in sculpture, in the figures of Neptune, Proserpina, David, Apollo and Daphne, and more minutely in some of the portrait busts already referred to. The rarity is when Bernini does not show movement in a work. How could we expect anything else from a vitalistic, naturalistic conception of reality in which life is an ever-changing process, and man, ideally at least, a creature of action, love, and hope who passes through death to new life?

But movement is a transitory and elusive phenomenon. For Bernini, artistic expressions of movement are not literal but illusionistic. Herbert Read draws a distinction between two kinds of illusionistic movement, essentially a symbolic kind in which the repetition of forms 'so stimulates the mind that an hallucinatory sensation is set up,' and a more specifically visual kind in which there is movement 'within the statue itself.' Starting from there, one might usefully stretch the distinction to include Bernini's

96

abstract symbols of movement. Read uses as an instance of the first, quite symbolic movement, the rippling effect of the tunics and skirts on the maidens of the Parthenon frieze. The equivalent in Bernini is the pure abstraction of the marble designs and of the structural and decorative details of his architecture, in this chapel and elsewhere. The emphasis here is on every sort of non-representational, often repetitive feature of design. The second, more intrinsic kind of movement (illustrated in Read by Bernini's *Apollo and Daphne*) is in the vibrant figure of Teresa, the seraph, and the chapel's other human or humanized forms caught in various gestures or actions.[67] But the two kinds of movement often fuse. In Teresa herself the simulated motion suggested in the features combines with the slightly chaotic repetition of the folds of material which the eye turns into rhythmic movement.

Both kinds occur abundantly in the chapel and are very skilfully fused into a total effect of movement. There is the abstract movement generated by marble patterns, running borders, and upward-inclining lines of the architecture, and there is the intrinsic movement of forms taken from nature – the clouds and wings – as well as the all-important human forms manifested as man, woman, skeleton, and angel. Distinctively baroque as the work is, individual manifestations of movement are so lucid within the total effect that they recall the words which Bernini used, through Chantelou's translation, to describe a Lebrun ceiling design: *abondance sans confusion*. The chapel is no cosmic diagram on the wall but a moving, evolving plan of God in which death and ecstasy are agents of change.

Behind all the manifestations two motives are discernible: movement as release, and movement as rising. Both bespeak an art whose meaning is free and open, an art of exuberance, elation, and marvellous transcendence. Bernini is excited by the possibility of possessing Teresa's true nature and giving it permanent existence. As Baldinucci remarks, had Bernini not given life to his sculptural figures, they 'might have remained mute and solitary in the native rock.' He could see Bernini's God-given, God-directed vitality expending itself in devotional acts of creation: 'It appeared from his eyes that he wanted his spirit to give life to the stone.'[68]

In this self-abrogating process he appears to take on the obligation of

XXVI Aeneas, Anchises, and Ascanius, rear view

freeing Man and Nature from earthly restrictions. That is what he does with marble faces, figures, and whole compositions. While Borromini gave flexibility to stone in the 'modelling' of buildings, Bernini did the same with sculpture. For Borromini it is an elastic material, for Bernini a malleable material he could fashion into a palm tree ruffled and bent by relentless southern winds.[69] He went as far as transforming men into spirits, and water into unusual physical forms. His fluid conception of reality resembles that of John Donne who, with a similar kind of ingenuity, shows the flow, change, and interfusion of all earthly things by converting water into solid ice or airy steam.

According to Baldinucci, Bernini knew from the beginning that his first talent was for sculpture, and it is relevant that 'his painting was merely a diversion.'[70] Critics commonly emphasize Bernini's visual bias, however. In the sense that Greek and western sculptors before Rodin, Maillol, and Henry Moore did not conscientiously exploit such sculptural properties of marble as its mass and volume, Bernini may not be a sculptural sculptor.[71] Yet that must not blind us to Bernini's genuinely sculptural qualities. As Henry Moore readily allows, truth to material is no measure of a work's value. In making sculpture serve the art of illusion Bernini commits himself not to truth of material but mastery over it. The depth and feel of many figures, and the design of many settings, are sculptural in effect. The complete meaning comes out of the Aeneas, Apollo, and Pluto groups, the Fountain of the Four Rivers, and many other works, only if they are seen as sculpture.

His ideas about working marble did not end where Michelangelo's ultimately did, with the conviction that a statue should seem to emerge from its confinement in stone. Bernini's devotion to lifelikeness led to the opposite result of making his figures look modelled rather than carved. Teresa and the seraph seem to be built up out of clay, little by little, rather than hewn out of marble blocks. The sheer skill with which he carved delicate forms has been widely admired, in the laurel fingers of Daphne, the swoop of Apollo's mantle, and the fine work, almost like filigree, which went into the carving of lace and curls. And intelligence of conception always accompanied his extraordinary technical skill, as in the carving of the flesh and muscles on the backs of Aeneas, Anchises, and Ascanius, which stands forever as an image of three human generations (PLATE XXVI). It was Stendhal's extravagant opinion that no Greek chisel produced anything to equal the head of St Teresa.[72]

Close study of the busts alone shows the long, careful planning which characterizes his work. While Bernini is not to be classed as one of the great Renaissance thinkers, his artistic intelligence has sometimes been underestimated.[73] His contentment lay in the work itself and he had no new theory of art to present. He took pleasure in making created things lose their weight and rise, move, spring, or fly. Hence the snakes piled coiling and squirming on Medusa's head and Daphne's hair blowing out behind her (which Bernini boasted about to Chantelou more than forty years after he carved it). Hence the grandiose illusionistic trick of raising mammoth bulks of marble or bronze on triflingly small bases – Constantine on the slight shanks of his rearing horse, the Four Rivers obelisk on a precariously cut-away base, the Cathedra Petri and its setting on the four extended fingers of four Church Fathers.

When Bernini's world gains its freedom and finds its unity, the movement is heavenward. In the chapel the propensity to rise is apparent in the animated skeletons, the arcing, flowing motion of the polychrome marbles, the rising confluence of the light beams, and the floating and flying angels in the frieze by the pediment and up in the celestial vault. Even the massive architectural frame, which by its nature seems least inclined to rise, loses some of its weight to the upward-thrusting columns and the opened lines of the pediment top. Active forces within the frame also give it a degree of buoyancy and lift – the seraph's large wings, the clouds beneath Teresa and inside the pediment triangle, the winged heads of *putti* ready to fly out of the broken pediment (PLATES V and IX). If the *putti* which first appeared in fifteenth-century painting were Renaissance 'symbols of the freedom we cannot win,' these of Bernini prefigure the freedom of heaven.[74]

In the upper part of the chapel just under the vault a considerable number of figured friezes and decorative borders are active and vibrant in the light, comparable in effect to what Wölfflin calls 'the flicker of a church façade' (PLATE IX). Except at the top, where they press urgently upwards on both sides of Teresa's image in the window, their direction is horizontal (PLATE XX). Yet angel forms, ribbons, wings, and fragments of abstract design break away (PLATE XIX). It is as though these rapid, repetitive, rhythmic bits might fly off in a dozen directions if not controlled by the upward movement of the ecstasy.

By a double metamorphosis well suited to the event, the seraph which is humanized and the saint who is etherealized both appear on the same high level, both affected by the fire of love. Can it be that this *concetto* of fire is present without being present? Fire as fire never appears. Yet symbols of fire, attributes of fire, and suggestions of fire, flame and flicker in various parts of the chapel, rising with the spiritual surge of the chapel – indeed within it, for fire is its vital force.

The seraph as St Teresa describes him is reproduced with as much exactness as Bernini's art allowed:

> . . . not tall, but short, and very beautiful, his face so aflame that
> he appeared to be one of the highest types of angel who seem
> to be all afire. . . . In his hands I saw a long golden spear and
> at the end of the iron tip I seemed to see a point of fire.

For a figure simulated although seeming to be real the seraph is executed with less literalness than in a vision, and his golden dart requires no 'point of fire.' But instead the seraphic mantle turns his body into one great twist of rising flame (PLATE II). His wings, half outstretched and ready for flight, seem to be feathered with flame, hints of which recur in the upward curling locks of his hair like tiny tongues of flame (PLATE XXIII). And perhaps the same tongues of flame are repeated again still higher, in the acanthus leaves of the Corinthian capitals above him and out at the corners of the chapel (PLATE IX). Beneath the figures, at the base of the frame and extending as a continuous line across the entire front of the chapel, a narrow fringe of flame licks upwards toward the ecstatic event.

The saint herself is a figure of fire – 'he left me completely afire with a great love of God.' She is partly enveloped in flamelike folds of material gathered at her throat (PLATE XXIV). In the grip of the rapture she meets the seraph with her soul, and her body appears to be falling away, as if to release the soul encased within it. Not until the time of resurrection will body and soul, parted by death, be united again. 'Sometimes the soul seems to be on the point of leaving the body,' says St Teresa, but only in death, for in ecstasy it never quite happens. In this ecstatic climax does Bernini in fact depict a rapturous death or a mystical moment of eternity? Perhaps both, but it is Crashaw, not Bernini, who shows Teresa going through the narrow pass from life to after-life.

The marble surfaces of Teresa's robes, modelled and lighted as they are, look like molten lava or thick wax running off her frame (PLATE XXI). The heavy folds of material drag her down. Her posture, like her clothing, appears to be melting away. Her hands and arms do nothing to sustain her. Had her body normal physical weight, she would drop down through the cloud. But she does not. On the testimony of our eyes her weight is sustained only by the loose fold of material held between the seraph's two fingers. As she is melted by the inner flame it seems possible that by this small means the seraph could lift her and carry her off.

In his late works Bernini expresses the force of rising by the tension created between horizontal and vertical lines. Here the lines are diagonal, and the lift comes from the energy of their jagged rising. No clear outline of the central group can emerge because the high ridges, deep-carved crevices, and glancing light effectively obscure it. But the main rising lines which define the two figures touch and overlap, the polished surfaces uniting into a single form. When seen at a distance with the light of the eye a little dimmed, the two figures are one shimmering flame-shape beginning at Teresa's extended foot, rising, and broadening into two large tongues of fire. Their union, expressed in the *Vida* as the fire of Divine Love, is delicately strengthened by the seraph's hand reaching out to touch her (PLATE XXVII).

The first time Bernini carved fire into sculptural form was in making flames curl up around the writhing body of St Lawrence on the grill. The treatment is tentative and quite literal, its effectiveness far less than the flaming cloaks with which he later clothed Daniel and the Angel with the Superscription. The sophisticated and more complex use of fire in the Teresan chapel advances the awesome Christian motive of showing the ultimate union of flesh and spirit. Though Bernini devoted the remaining thirty years of his life mainly to religious subjects, including statues of saints, he never again produced a saint in ecstasy. It was his most successful re-creation of mystical experience and he had no more to say.

With age he became increasingly devout. His late life was scarcely less turbulent than Michelangelo's. As he lay in bed feeling plagued by

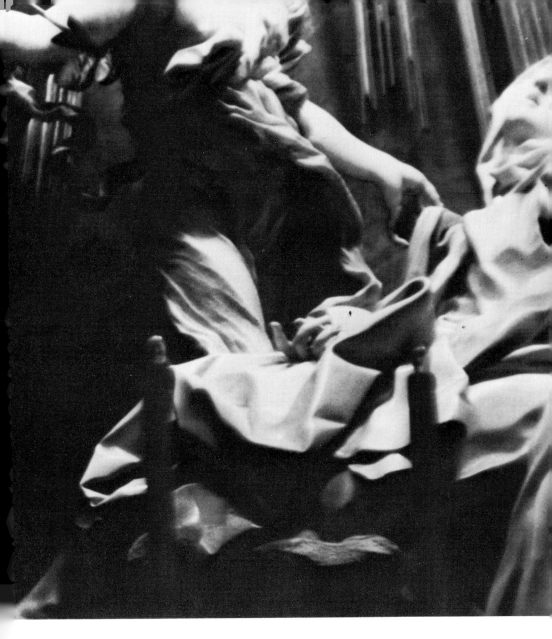

XXVII St Teresa and the Seraph, middle section

religious scruples, he kept continually before him a painting of the crucified Christ from whose wounds flowed blood enough to flood the earth.[75] Preternaturally strong until his last illness, Bernini worked at his sculpture tirelessly, sometimes for seven hours at a time, and always with someone at hand to prevent him from falling off the scaffolding. He worked as if in a trance, and when an assistant urged him to stop and rest, the reply was, 'Let me alone. I am in love.'[76]

Part III

Text of Crashaw's Hymn

A Hymn to the Name and Honor of the Admirable Saint Teresa

*In memory of the virtuous and learned lady Madre de Teresa that sought
an early martyrdom*

Love, thou art absolute sole lord
Of life and death. To prove the word,
We'll now appeal to none of all
Those thy old soldiers, great and tall,
Ripe men of martyrdom, that could reach down,   5
With strong arms, their triumphant crown;
Such as could with lusty breath
Speak loud into the face of death
Their great Lord's glorious name – to none
Of those whose spacious bosoms spread a throne   10
For love at large to fill: spare blood and sweat,
And see him take a private seat,
Making his mansion in the mild
And milky soul of a soft child.
   Scarce hath she learned to lisp the name   15
Of martyr, yet she thinks it shame
Life should so long play with that breath
Which spent can buy so brave a death.
She never undertook to know
What death with love should have to do,   20
Nor has she e'er yet understood
Why to show love, she should shed blood
Yet though she cannot tell you why,

She can love, and she can die.
    Scarce hath she blood enough to make   25
A guilty sword blush for her sake;
Yet hath she a heart dares hope to prove
How much less strong is death than love.
Be love but there, let poor six years
Be posed with[a] the maturest fears   30
Man trembles at, you straight shall find
Love knows no nonage, nor the mind.
'Tis love, not years nor limbs, that can
Make the martyr or the man.
    Love touched her heart, and lo it beats   35
High, and burns with such brave heats,
Such thirsts to die, as dares drink up
A thousand cold deaths in one cup.
Good reason, for she breathes all fire.
Her weak breast heaves with strong desire   40
Of what she may with fruitless wishes
Seek for amongst her mother's kisses.
    Since 'tis not to be had at home
She'll travel for a martyrdom.
No home for her[b] confesses she   45
But where she may a martyr be.
    She'll to the Moors and trade[c] with them,
For this unvalued[d] diadem.
She'll offer them her dearest breath,
With Christ's name in't, in change for death.   50
She'll bargain with them, and will give
Them God, teach them how to live
In him; or if they this deny,
For him she'll teach them how to die.

[a] stand opposed to
[b] her 1646/hers 1648
[c] trade 1646/try 1648
[d] beyond price

So shall she leave amongst them sown   55
Her Lord's blood, or at least her own.
   Farewell then, all the world! Adieu!
Teresa is no more for you.
Farewell, all pleasures, sports, and joys,
(Never till now esteemèd toys).   60
Farewell whatever dear may be,
Mother's arms or father's knee.
Farewell house and farewell home!
She's for the Moors and martyrdom.
   Sweet, not so fast! Lo thy fair spouse   65
Whom thou seekst with so swift vows,
Calls thee back, and bids thee come,
T'embrace a milder martyrdom.
   Blest pow'rs forbid thy tender life
Should bleed upon a barb'rous knife;   70
Or some base hand have pow'r to race[e]
Thy breast's chaste[f] cabinet, and uncase
A soul kept there so sweet. O no,
Wise heav'n will never have it so.
Thou art love's victim and must die   75
A death more mystical and high.
Into love's arms thou shalt let fall
A still-surviving funeral.
His is the dart must make the death
Whose stroke shall taste thy hallowed breath;   80
A dart thrice dipped in that rich flame
Which writes thy spouse's radiant name
Upon the roof of heav'n, where aye
It shines, and with a sov'reign ray
Beats bright upon the burning faces   85
Of souls which in that name's sweet graces
Find everlasting smiles. So rare,

[e] slash or slit
[f] chaste 1646/soft 1648

109

So spiritual, pure, and fair
Must be th'immortal instrument
Upon whose choice point shall be sent   90
A life so loved. And that there be
Fit executioners for thee,
The fair'st and first-born sons of fire,
Blest seraphim, shall leave their choir
And turn love's soldiers, upon thee   95
To exercise their archery.
    O how oft shalt thou complain
Of a sweet and subtle pain!
Of intolerable joys!
Of a death in which who dies   100
Loves his death, and dies again,
And would forever so be slain!
And lives and dies and knows not why
To live, but that he thus may never leave to die.
    How kindly will thy gentle heart   105
Kiss the sweetly-killing dart!
And close in thine embraces keep
Those delicious wounds that weep
Balsam to heal themselves with. Thus
When these thy deaths so numerous,   110
Shall all at last die into one,
And melt thy soul's sweet mansion,
Like a soft lump of incense, hasted
By too hot a fire, and wasted
Into perfuming clouds, so fast   115
Shalt thou exhale to heav'n at last
In a resolving sigh, and then –
O what? Ask not the tongues of men.
Angels cannot tell. Suffice
Thy self shall feel thine own full joys   120
And hold them fast forever. There
So soon as thou shalt first appear,
The moon of maiden stars, thy white

Mistress, attended by such bright
Souls as thy shining self, shall come 125
And in her first ranks make thee room,
Where 'mongst her snowy family
Immortal welcomes wait for thee.
    O what delight, when revealed life shall stand
And teach thy lips heav'n with her hand, 130
On which thou now maist to thy wishes
Heap up thy consecrated kisses.
What joys shall seize thy soul when she,
Bending her blessed eyes on thee
(Those second smiles of heav'n), shall dart 135
Her mild rays through thy melting heart!
    Angels, thy old friends, there shall greet thee,
Glad at their own home now to meet thee.
    All thy good works which went before
And waited for thee at the door, 140
Shall own thee there; and all in one
Weave a constellation
Of crowns, with which the King thy spouse
Shall build up thy triumphant brows.
All thy old woes shall now smile on thee, 145
And thy pains sit bright upon thee,
All thy sorrows here shall shine,
And thy sufferings be divine.
Tears shall take comfort and turn gems,
And wrongs repent to diadems. 150
Ev'n thy deaths shall live, and new
Dress the soul that erst they slew.
Thy wounds shall blush to such bright scars
As keep account of the Lamb's wars.
    Those rare works where thou shalt leave writ 155
Love's noble history, with wit
Taught thee by none but him, while here
They feed our souls, shall clothe thine there.
Each heav'nly word by whose hid flame

III

Our hard hearts shall strike fire, the same   160
Shall flourish on thy brows, and be
Both fire to us, and flame to thee –
Whose light shall live bright in thy face
By glory, in our hearts by grace.
   Thou shalt look round about, and see   165
Thousands of crowned souls throng to be
Themselves thy crown, sons of thy vows,
The virgin-births with which thy sov'reign spouse
Made fruitful thy fair soul. Go now,
And with them all about thee, bow   170
To him. Put on (he'll say) put on
My rosy love – that thy rich zone[g]
Sparkling with the sacred flames
Of thousand souls, whose happy names
Heav'n keeps upon thy score. (Thy bright   175
Life brought them first to kiss the light
That kindled them to stars.) And so
Thou with the Lamb, thy Lord, shalt go,
And whereso'er he sets his white
Steps, walk with him those ways of light   180
Which who[h] in death would live to see,
Must learn in life to die like thee.[77]

[g] girdle or belt
[h] whoever

Part IV

Crashaw's Ascent Beyond Time

One

Baroque Abundance

At the Vatican, as early as the 1620's, Bernini contrived a glorious firmament which shone with the light of two thousand lamps hidden behind illusionistic clouds. For the pre-Lenten Carnivale of 1637 it is said that he produced something called the *Comedy of Two Theatres* – a baffling creation in which the spectators watched not only the performance but a reflection of themselves watching. Sometimes a *fantasia* of that kind, combining dramatic action, scenery, dancing, music, words, and stage machinery, was produced entirely by Bernini. On occasion he spent a whole month acting out all the parts of a play he was to direct. Although he did not invent the stage machinery for which he is commonly given credit, his artful use of it added a new illusionistic dimension to the baroque theatre by actively involving the audience. His special effects, like buildings falling and the Tiber flooding over, filled people with terror, and so did an artificial fire he contrived for the stage – artificial yet frighteningly believable, for it was his purpose to expose the spectator to so many conflicting visions of reality that he would become delightfully lost in the confusion.[78]

Of course Bernini's major accomplishments were in sculpture and architecture. But he also made fair claim to being a painter (of an unknown number of works), playwright, designer (of frontispieces for books), engineer-planner (of the arsenal at Civitavecchia and fortifications in the Borgo), and in addition was the designer and decorator of many diverse things – catafalques, processional cars, crucifixes, eagles, andirons, picture frames. In connection with Queen Christina's arrival in Rome, for example, he decorated the Porta del Popolo; designed for her a 'royal seat' and a large mirror with a figure of Truth; cast in painted and gilded sugar a double-allegory of Minerva and Abundance in elaborate scenes; and adorned with sky-blue velvet and silver fittings the carriage used for her formal entrance into the city.[79]

If it were possible to isolate one trait of Bernini's artistry which expresses his thoughts, his desires, and the bent of his genius, it would be the sculptural trait. Whether classicized or freely baroque, whether a building, statue, painting, drawing, clay *bozzetto*, or ephemeral construction, each characteristic work was shaped, elaborated, and unified, as a body in space. Aside from Titian and perhaps Correggio, the painters who influenced him most strongly were all very sculptural: the early Reni, the late Annibale Carracci, and Raphael, whom he placed first among painters.[80] Especially in his early work he was deeply influenced by Roman sculpture, and always by his artistic ideal Michelangelo, who showed him how to understand the human form and much more. In actual practice Bernini saw plastic and pictorial representation as one, but his manner of developing a subject by rounding it and proliferating it into a scenic unit was unmistakably sculptural.

In the declining days of the *uomo universale* when versatility for its own sake was a fading ideal, it was belief which gave coherence to most of Bernini's work. The same could be said of the English poet Richard Crashaw (1613?-1649), though the personalities and lives have almost nothing else in common. Crashaw may have been more profoundly religious, at least in the sense that he came to his Catholic faith out of a foreign culture, craved it, cut all ties for it. As against Bernini's relatively outgoing, highly successful and gratifying life of eighty-two years Crashaw's was the brief life of a troubled man in troubled times, a man born in the wrong place, living there honourably, quietly, introvertedly, then finally following his soul 'home' to the continent. (In his poetry the word 'home' generally means the soul's resting place.) In Bernini faith joyously deepened and beautified creation, which is deity's manifestation. The tragic sense, that awareness of conflict between human and transcendental values, was not in him. For quite another reason it was not in Crashaw either, since as time passed he seems more and more to have left people and wordly affairs behind him. He preferred above all else the sublimity of faith and poetry. As the mystical flame which warmed and consumed him was generally absent in other English divines, their moral concern and their 'practical strenuousness' were absent in him.[81]

The people he favoured most were women, a very extraordinary group of women: the Virgin Mother, a saint (Teresa), a queen who shared his faith (Henrietta Maria), the high-principled and celibate 'mother' of Little Gidding (Mary Collett), and a devout friend and patroness (the Countess of Denbigh). Since this sternly pious and disciplined man was apparently more closely connected to them than to Christ, St Thomas Aquinas, or his poet friends Abraham Cowley and Joseph Beaumont (Thomas Car may be the exception), the psychoanalyst's view, and Goethe's, would doubtless be that Crashaw spent his short life searching for his mother or mothers. In them he presumably found comfort, beauty, freedom, inspiration, and his haven of faith. The Catholic son of a rabid Puritan, he found himself in a country which from his point of view was fighting the wrong religious war. The hard journey to the mother church was over broken road, but it was the only journey he could take.

In contrast to Bernini's Roman expressiveness, Crashaw's introversion and his well-educated English reticence make him ultimately unknowable. We see sudden bursts of light, but they do not show the whole man. Compared to Bernini's, his artistic output was smaller, less varied, and, one is inclined to say, less public and grand. But it must be remembered that Bernini was not always public and grand, and that Crashaw, in a different artistic idiom, holds a vast, transcendental subject within the tight compass of his art. Well-read, highly proficient in many languages, at odds with the world, in his late days the perfect likeness of a ragged, world-weary anchorite whose eyes flashed with divine fire, Crashaw was very unlike Bernini. He was one of England's important poets, though not one of its greatest – and as we shall see, not entirely English either.

Though poetry is the only art in which Crashaw gained distinction, he had others. The anonymous preface to his book of poems called *Steps to the Temple* says he was accomplished in 'music, drawing, limning, graving.'[82] Besides painting original subjects he copied several portraits and did illustrations and engravings, including a number of engravings for his posthumously published volume, *Carmen Deo Nostro*.[83] But as the same preface says, Crashaw took poetry to be 'the grand business of his soul' and let the other arts be 'subservient recreations for vacant hours.' Whatever he may have done with music, painting comes into his poetry as both a subject and a metaphor. His last poem on St Teresa,

'The Flaming Heart,' instructs a painter to give the veil to the seraph and put the dart in Teresa's hand. But Crashaw's talent for the visual arts, and his sophistication in that direction, seem finally to have been nothing remarkable. One sometimes forgets that cultivated Englishmen of Crashaw's day, with a handful of exceptions, thought of painting and portraiture as roughly synonymous, and that England had no major, native-born painter before Hogarth.

At the same time, painting and music are conspicuously present in his poetry, though less as subjects than as principles affecting his style. Poets are symbolic artists who cannot choose to be representational. The immediate sensation of poetry may be visual, yet it is obvious that the direct visual experience of printed words on a page is little more than the stimulus for the vastly larger indirect experience which follows. Forms which might be interpreted almost directly by the sculptor must be completely broken down and remade into language by the poet – and that phase only begins the flow of sensuous and mental responses which complete the poetic experience.

In seventeenth-century English poetry, which is a high peak in the literature, vision itself goes off the object. At that time neither English poets nor the majority of continental poets were good *direct* observers of man and nature. Their intentions lay elsewhere. No lover Donne addresses can be visually imagined; he looks through her eyes to the inside. Herbert's grapes and Vaughan's waterfall are not seen; Crashaw's 'Supposed Mistress' never emerges from the poetic paradise; and Marvell's 'Coy Mistress' is a lady whose features leap toward infinity. In looking at nature Marvell and Vaughan transform it into idea and feeling, in somewhat the way Saint-Amant, Tristan L'Hermite, and other foreign poets do, but Donne merely ignores it. Crashaw's love of Spenser was not an emulation of Spenser's talent for precise visual observation, since in religious poetry vision turns inward and upward (the two are usually the same). For his part Crashaw carries the tendency toward indirect vision as far as it can go. Like Herbert, and not only Herbert, he seems sometimes to have begun with a kind of icon – an emblem, crucifix, picture, or other visual object – and then to have converted it into a completely new experience. However, Crashaw's musical ear always conditioned the visual experience on its way to becoming a poem.

Among the six or eight senses which exist,[84] the one which gives his poetry distinctiveness is hearing. As a poet Crashaw is strongly musical, not because he calls his poems 'songs,' 'hymns,' and *Carmen*, not in the sense of dealing directly with music (although he makes a broad display of musical terms and concepts in 'Music's Duel'), but in the sense of making poetic sound and poetic rhythm constantly effective in his poetry. He has been called the most ambitious musician of the Metaphysical group.[85] He was different from Milton and Dryden, who deliberately made some of their poetry *sound* like music, and more like Bernini, in making musical qualities function in an art where everything is 'simulated although seeming to be real.' In precision, delicacy, and resiliency of use, Crashaw's ear is one of the best in English poetry. As Bernini is sculptural, Crashaw is 'musical.' Yet there is more to Crashaw's music than this gift of ear which deepens the musical quality of the poetry. There is the magnificent suitability of music to his main poetic theme.

Men cannot taste or touch or see divinity as well as they can hear it. In the process of refining, subliming, and elevating, different kinds of sensations are involved, and all of them combine and interfuse in a struggle for transcendence. In a strictly Christian sense Crashaw is probably the most mystical of English poets, and in part because his verses aspire to the abstraction, energy, and harmony of music. 'Your ports are all superfluous here, / Save that which lets in faith, the ear,' he says, and in another mood, 'Go, smiling souls, your new-built cages break, / In heav'n you'll learn to sing. . . .' In Crashaw's poetry sound is divine evocation and ethereal echo, a celestial sense originating in the silent or inaudible world above. As everything human aspires to unity, human unity aspires to divine.

Quite understandably, the artistic uses to which sensation was put in Crashaw's time were not restrictively baroque but belonged to a unitive vision which was not uncommon even in a world of war and change. Though no style of the age is more conspicuous than the Baroque, the word is not synonymous with the age. It flourished mainly in the Catholic world of south and central Europe, was taken up in parts of the German north, intruded somewhat on the classical consciousness of France, and never prevailed in England. But that unitive vision had at least two characteristics expressive of late-Renaissance art and relevant to both Crashaw and

Bernini: the enormous production of fused art forms, and the prominence of synesthesia in the artistic idiom of the times.[86]

The phenomenon or practice of treating sensory material synesthetically, that is to say, of describing one sensation in terms of another (Gombrich calls it 'a splashing over of impressions from one sense modality to another'), though familiar in many eras and in everyday life, is especially evident in art.[87] One sense satisfies another, is exchanged for another or enlarges another, even in such simple verbal instances as a bitter wind, a blue mood, or the silent moon of Milton's *Samson Agonistes*. And it often happens that synesthesia develops, as it does with Crashaw, into a 'logic of spirit' which contradicts physical law and natural experience, as in the words 'the dart must make the death / Whose stroke shall taste thy hallowed breath.' What synaesthesia and fused forms insist on, implicitly, is the unity of all parts of man, and sometimes even the unity of his past, present, and future: the body of youth, mind of maturity, and soul of age all at once.

Consequently the borderlines between genres may melt away. The ordinary observer sees the architecture, painting, decoration, and relief sculpture of Bernini's chapel as co-extensive. As Marino observes in his *Dicerie Sacre*, one art exchanges with another its own peculiar quality. Poetry, he says, gains special excellence by assuming the voice and air of the kindred art of music. Here, according to Focillon, all arts pool their resources, cross the frontiers which separate them, and freely borrow effects from one another.[88] It is a revival of Simonides' idea of the poem as a speaking picture and the painting as a silent poem, and of Horace's *ut pictura poesis*. When Montaigne set himself the task of revealing himself in writing he said 'c'est moy que je *peins*.' In late-Renaissance art it was more common than usual to feel with the intellect and understand with the senses.

Thus the age invented or developed not only mixed forms like the Christian epic and English tragi-comedy which French classicism vehemently attacked as *mélange des genres*, but many others: ballet, opera, masque, emblem book, shaped verses, scenic oratorio, odes to music, *zarzuelas* (or musical comedies), as well as curiosities like the water organ, the colour piano, and music written expressly to please the eye. Ben Jonson and Inigo Jones conceive of the masque in the way Marino and others do the emblem: the picture is the 'body,' the word the 'soul.' The emblem, called by Francis Quarles a 'silent parable,' by a Lucan translator 'un art ingénieux de peindre la parole, et de parler aux yeux,' and by Giarda, a hieroglyph of divine reality, had wide acceptance among poets in many countries. Its impact was felt in England not only by Crashaw but by Marlowe, Webster, Spenser, Shakespeare, Jonson, Herbert, Marvell, Milton, and others. Indeed emblems and a few manuals of myth, from Ovid's (called 'the Painter's Bible') to those of Ripa, Tritonio, and Lomazzo, account for most of the figures of allegory and personification in the writing of the age. Crashaw's poetry of music and Bernini's *bel composto* in the Cornaro Chapel may not be blood relations to the emblem, but again, whether in witty or cosmically serious expressions, the unitive vision which shows through the emblem and other forms is also in their vision.

While in many respects Crashaw and Bernini are worlds apart, both expressed themselves in the style we now call 'baroque.' In Focillon's opinion, though the Baroque is but a moment in the long life of artistic evolution, it was the most emancipated and fully expressive moment we know of in the past. Baroque forms, he says,

> live with passionate intensity a life that is entirely their own; they proliferate like some vegetable monstrosity. They break apart even as they grow; they tend to invade space in every direction, to perforate it, to become as one with all its possibilities.[89]

If it were possible to describe the baroque outlook in a sentence perhaps it would be that the Baroque embraces total reality, reconciles its opposing forces, and sees the life of man as passing, as becoming, as always flowing into the future. This last was anticipated by Montaigne's very method of writing the *Essais*: 'je ne peins pas l'estre, je peins le passage.' As distinguished from this broad approximation of the baroque outlook, baroque art expresses a range of characteristics too numerous and various to be easily written down. Although a case could be made for calling Bernini's St Teresa and its chapel *the* typical baroque work, it is no more possible than to call any one nineteenth-century piece *the* typical Romantic work. That the characteristics of Baroque are sometimes contradictory as well as numerous is suggested by Wellek's distinction between two forms of baroque literature, essentially the mystical and introverted, and the courtly and public which continues the traditions of Petrarchism and rhetorical humanism.[90] If the centre of the term 'Baroque' cannot be located exactly, neither can its circumference be drawn, for the word itself has a reality which was invented only after the fact. But, hypothetically at least, between the centre and the circumference lie a number of familiar characteristics of Baroque which can be noted, all of them somewhere apparent to the viewer looking back at Bernini's work and forward now to Crashaw's. Should we conceive of a baroque omniwork it might embody, on the formal level: unity of composition (in which figures and environment tend to merge), immensity of conception and often of scale, unsymmetrical balance (expressive of the baroque preference for what one perceives over what one knows to exist), multiplicity of related or relatable parts, complexity of time reference (frequently related to the frame of eternity), openness of form (since nature and the cosmos commonly interfuse), and, as against formal regularity, the slightly irregular elements of form (a penchant for curves, rhythmic variations, and definite but imperfect patterns) which resemble actuality. And on the expressive level, which in fact is not separable from the other: intricacy of invention (to convey the paradox, wit, and discovery of actual experience), imagery of fluency and change (as it expresses the human condition), symbolic and metaphorical 'language' (to reveal the realities beyond perception), a dramatic, quasi-dramatic, or rhetorical manner (to involve the perceiver), and — by no means least important — the intensity and movement generated by an enormous amount of spiritual and emotional energy.

But even though the Baroque was the dominant artistic idiom of seventeenth-century Europe, it was, as we recall, much less than all of Europe, and as an art style no one feature of it belongs uniquely to that epoch. Given the conditions of war, the shifting of frontiers, centres of power and social classes, given the clash between the Old Faith and the New Philosophy, the seventeenth century was more emphatically than usual a new age. On the broad scene radical artistic innovations were frequent (if seldom entirely detached from the past), and in art there appeared new forms and new subjects. Europe, especially southern

Europe, saw new saints and martyrs appearing, or familiar ones newly interpreted, with the repentant Magdalene seeming to lead the way. There and elsewhere allegories began to burgeon, on scriptural and also non-scriptural topics; genre painting discovered new objects and methods; the commonplace, vernacular voice was heard, and the everyday figure was seen; nature came into its own with sea, land, and sky for the first time becoming subjects of art in their own right.

To this general scene Crashaw relates only awkwardly. As a poet he is the one figure we may call 'Baroque' and 'Metaphysical' at once – and his case aptly shows the entanglement of these kindred terms.[91] Writing about Crashaw the 'Metaphysical poet' in the 1920's, T. S. Eliot placed him in the mainstream of English poetry, but since then, with the advance of the term 'Baroque,' Crashaw has become the only English poet to whom the word is applied without challenge. Although in certain lights Crashaw looks very un-English, today we can fairly call him the most baroque of English poets.

If the meanings of 'Metaphysical' and 'Baroque' were not so indistinct in outline one could almost say that baroque poetry is an image super-imposed on the image of Metaphysical poetry, with not much individual difference left on either side. Henry Vaughan's 'bodied ideas' and Donne's phrase 'naked thinking heart' or his assertion 'one might almost say her body thought' quite closely resemble thought and wording in Théophile de Viau, Marino, Schirmer, and other 'continental baroque' poets. Both are included in Eliot's ideas of 'sensuous thought' and 'of thinking through the senses, or of senses thinking.'[92] Yet areas exist where distinctions can sometimes be drawn. In imagery baroque poetry is generally richer, more sensuous, more fantastic, and more often purely secular than Metaphysical poetry, while the latter, in both form and thought is usually a more intellectualized, careful, and finished poetry.

Since the Metaphysicals were not a school but a number of poets who wrote in the same place, time, and tradition, to take Donne as their exemplar is a convenience which neglects much of the truth. Yet if we think of Donne developing poems intellectually, analytically, and intricately, in order to internalize experience, we begin to see how Crashaw is associated with both Metaphysical and Baroque. Crashaw's mode of internalizing is quite different from Donne's, the difference between intellectualized passion and spiritualized passion. While Crashaw's interest in life of the intellect is minimal, his attraction to the spiritual passion of Catholic Baroque is limitless. 'As lines so loves oblique may well / Themselves in every angle greet' are Marvell's words, and they could be Donne's, but not Crashaw's. He more closely resembles Marino, Huygens, and D'Aubigné among writers, and Gaulli and Murillo among painters, than he does any writer or painter in England. Many readers have been surprised to learn that his imagery and manner of thinking, far from being individually eccentric, are just those which abound in continental baroque literature and art. For different reasons, Hopkins disliked his poetry and Pope thought his art strained and his ideas far-fetched. Those who liked him best were writers of a specific kind of exuberance, often Romantic exuberance, including Shelley, Swinburne, and Emerson, and to a degree Coleridge, who had Crashaw in mind during the writing of the second part of 'Cristabel.'[93]

Spiritually removed from England even before he left it, Crashaw treated the subject of Christ, for example, not with the English concern for His power of redemption but with a baroque emphasis on Christ's presence in man's life, Christ of the Incarnation and the Passion. Crashaw would not pass for a European poet either. He had a voice of his own, at home very foreign in tone, and abroad very foreign in sound. His Marino translation is not an authentic Marino poem. Yet Marino's aim in poetry was *la meraviglia*, the very wonder, awe, and astonishment which Crashaw transforms into spiritual sublimity. Although Francis Thompson's estimate of Crashaw is anything but friendly it comes very close: a man attracted to religious themes not for their lessons but their beauty and grandeur. 'In other words, he hymns but does not preach; hails, but does not expound.'[94]

In Crashaw we await the meaning, only to discover eventually that it is worked out not as a conclusion but as a luminous path of revelation. The poetry combines an extraordinary amount of emotional intensity with an extraordinary purity of spirit. Its secret probably lies just there, in the union of sensation and spirit. One critic says his mysticism begins in sense perception, the next that his images are not sense images. The actuality is more elusive and unusual.

If sensations are understood as much more than bodily responses, Crashaw is a poet of sensations rather than a sensuous poet. His most passionate statements are in the sacred poems, not the secular, which are generally conventional and occasional. At times he leads us to expect extremely sensuous poetry, with titles like 'On the bleeding wounds of our crucified Christ' and 'Upon the body of our blessed Lord, naked and bloody,' but the expectation is not fulfilled. His most passionate feelings avoid the impression of being self-indulgent or auto-intoxicating because they are directed toward God, not himself. The external world seems to exist only dimly. In fact he is at his most grotesque and tasteless when his internal vision really loses connection with external vision, as when Mary's bosom is a nest of Love's fires and floods and her breasts are sister-seas of virgin milk. But when he describes Christ's wounds as eyes and mouths, and Mary drinking from her son's bleeding breasts, he is sensuous and more than sensuous. 'A cruel and costly spring' (echoed in Eliot) is not a season but the weather within. Indeed, nearly all his favourite words are ambivalent. *Sweet, bright, soft, glad, gay, fragrant, rosy, purple,* and *golden* sink their sensuousness into states of spirit. Sensation is in the service of spirit. It is a 'sensuous thought' whose sublimity rises to a pitch rarely reached in poetry. Crashaw's extravagance is extravagance of faith, his sensuousness a sensuousness belonging to an elevated order of life where everything attains to perfectly intense purity of spirit.

It is here that the baroque sensibilities of Crashaw and Bernini begin to meet. Bernini painted Christ's wounds flooding the earth, and Crashaw wrote of Christ's wounds bleeding like rivers flowing to the Red Sea, like rivers becoming 'thy blood's deluge . . . a deluge of deliverance.' In Crashaw's poetry the Teresan ecstasy must necessarily be more remote, more inward, more abstract than Bernini's primarily visual presentation of it. But fluent, transcending movement belongs to both. Whatever words can do, whatever marble can show, there is more. Many seventeenth-century writers felt the limits of language. Donne, Herbert, Quevedo, and Johannes Plavius are among them. As Leo Spitzer once observed, the baroque writer 'says something with the full consciousness that one cannot actually say it. He knows all the difficulties of translation from intention to expression, the whole insufficiency of linguistic expression.' St Teresa herself, who also had this consciousness, taught

Crashaw that 'love is eloquence.' He found his own ways to show the human faculties merging in transcendence: 'eyes are vocal, tears have tongues,' there are 'sights not seen with eyes' and 'words . . . not heard with ears.' The equivalent in Bernini is the illusionistic act of relieving marble of its cold weight. Both men sacrifice art to meaning by burning up substance in spirit. In the cleansing fire Crashaw finds 'effectual whispers, whose still voice the soul itself feels more than hears.' This is the new eloquence of his ambition 'to climb upon the stoop'd shoulders of old Time, and trace Eternity.'

Emergence of the Poem

'A Hymn to the Name and Honor of the Admirable Saint Teresa,' one of Crashaw's three Teresan poems, first appeared in *Steps to the Temple* in 1646. As the first English poet honoured primarily as an ode writer, Crashaw begins a poetic tradition which flourished abundantly for over two centuries.[45] While it is fair to say that he wrote excellent poetry but seldom an excellent poem, 'A Hymn to . . . Saint Teresa' is his most accomplished, most fully developed work.

An Englishman by birth and training, Crashaw was well acquainted with biblical and classical literature, especially the Latin authors whom he knew well in his university days. He read Spenser, but also Sidney, Herbert, and very likely Jonson, Shakespeare, and Donne. As time passed he left the ancient authors behind and read more and more in Marino and Ceba, the Jesuits Strada, Remond, Bettinus, and Biderman, and many mystical writers including the Spanish.[96] The last were subjects for study, translation, and paraphrase. It was St Teresa's writing he knew best, however. From the anonymous preface to *Steps to the Temple* we know that he excelled in Hebrew, Greek, and Latin, and that he learned Italian and Spanish by himself. Different parts of her work had been widely translated and although two or three versions of the *Vida* were already accessible in English by 1645, Crashaw read it in Spanish.[97] The experience kindled his desire to make her 'speak English too,' as he says.[98] In short, this was a poet who gradually turned all his learning, reading, and thinking toward what Cowley, in his famous elegy to Crashaw, calls 'the boundless Godhead':

> Thou from low earth to nobler flames did rise,
> And like Elijah, mount alive the skies.

As the unrest of the Civil War continued in England, Crashaw at

Cambridge withdrew more and more into the church of Little St Mary's and his 'little contentful kingdom' of Peterhouse. Even today it is not sure that he ever took orders, but as either curate or a minor functionary at Little St Mary's, and as a fellow of Peterhouse, Crashaw lived a private life of severe piety, aloof from the life outside, leaving only for frequent retreats to Little Gidding. In 1644 he was ejected from his fellowship at Peterhouse and lost all his other privileges. By then his Catholic sentiments were sufficiently well known for him to be criticized as objectionably Roman in both doctrine and religious observance.[99] Yet he had been so successful a preacher that visitors thronged to hear him give sermons which, according to the chronicler David Lloyd, 'ravished more like poems.'

If we are to trust that same preface, Crashaw wrote the poems '*in* St Mary's Church,' and the fact is oddly revealing because they owe less to the sun of the day than to the dark quiet of night and strange brilliance of afterlife. In *Dark Night of the Soul* by St John of the Cross, Crashaw must have read with approval that the very light of divine wisdom is the soul's darkness because its brilliance so far exceeds anything the soul can comprehend. At that time Dowsing and his righteous group came through and destroyed much of the 'blasphemous' decoration in Cambridge, but in the church of Little St Mary's, under what remained of the cherub faces and 'roof of angels' adorning Peterhouse chapel, Crashaw re-animated the familiar mystical themes into fresh poetic experience. It was there that he filled an imaginative empire with wings and eyes and hearts and flames and blood, with sweetness and brightness, with dark rivers, purple wounds, rosy dawns, and maiden-white flesh. Plurals of the earth and sky melt in the oneness of divinity, phrases swell and multiply, clauses rise and strain until they break. 'A fever burns thee and Love lights the fire,' says Cowley. The passion of spirit which floods Crashaw's poetry seems to pull the lines away from earth, reason, and language itself.

For one thus separated from the England around him – removed from external experience as Bernini seldom was – the act of conversion had little effect on his style of life. He formally became a Roman Catholic in 1645 or early 1646, while still in England or soon after arriving in France. Since the change came gradually, over a period of years, it matters very little whether the 'Hymn to St Teresa' was written before or after he joined the Roman Church.[100] That religious conversion is no easier to explain than falling in love – least of all by those who are immediately involved – is a truism which applies. But some things are known about Crashaw's conversion, and others can be surmised. It is said that distrust of the senses is a trait which religious Englishmen inherited from Puritanism and Evangelicism. In this respect Crashaw was not typically English. Divine excitement and perfect quiet were states of soul more important to him than current ideas on religious conduct and church government. The quality of spiritual life always concerned him more than doctrinal dissatisfaction. In a disarmingly factual and partisan way, Anthony à Wood attributes Crashaw's change to his 'infallible foresight that the Church of England would be quite ruined by the unlimited fury of the Presbyterians.' However that may be, it was Crashaw's conviction that the Church of England wasted too much time defending reformed Catholicism against attacks by Puritans. But the essential motive was different: Crashaw had a zeal which sought the *unión mística* and he wished to join the company of mystics and saints.[101] St Teresa believed souls have no nationality. In Crashaw's case nationality, personality, and materiality all fell away with the rise of his spirit. Though it sounds extreme, the opinion of Yeats is substantially true, that Crashaw's Teresan ode is 'the most impersonal of ecstasies.'

Crashaw was a religious exile in Leyden for a brief time before he left England permanently. In Paris he lived mainly at the exile court of Queen Henrietta Maria in the Louvre. He must have taken satisfaction in belonging, along with the Queen, to a group sometimes called 'the cult of St Teresa.' But English Catholics were in an impoverished and anxious exile. Crashaw himself continued his ascetic existence, intensely devout and utterly negligent about everything earthly including the simple necessities of food and dress. Despite his respect for Henrietta Maria as royal queen and champion of Catholics, after about a year in Paris he left for Rome with her blessings in the fall of 1646. The end of his life was not far off. For part of the three years he spent in Rome he held a minor church post – the record is sketchy[102] – and then in the final weeks or months of his life he travelled to Loreto to take up a small benefice. By then he was extremely ill, possibly because of his arduous pilgrimage over the Apennines. A violent fever soon overtook him – the result, said David Lloyd, of 'the holy ardour of his soul overheating his body.' Cowley's account strikes a higher pitch:

> How well (blest swan) did Fate contrive thy death,
> And made thee render up thy tuneful breath
> In thy mistress' arms!

The three poems on St Teresa were finished before Crashaw reached Rome, excepting the famous closing lines of 'The Flaming Heart' which were added later. Published first in 1646, the poems were otherwise altered only slightly in the editions of 1648 and 1652. Since Bernini was working on the Cornaro Chapel when Crashaw was in Rome, many have been led to believe that he met Bernini or saw his work, but everything argues against it. Crashaw died in 1649 and the Cornaro Chapel was not opened until two years later. Moreover, while Crashaw makes no mention at all of Bernini or his work, he explicitly refers to Teresa's writing in all three of the poems: 'those rare works' and that 'bright book' are the Teresa he knew; 'the flame I took from reading thee' is his burning inspiration.[103]

The Hymn, which is longer than both the other poems together, gives the impression of being a saint's life in verse, but only on the surface. Crashaw aims to bring out the essence of Teresa's nature, not its accidents, not her narrative history. The three movements of the poem follow in order: Teresa's early quest for martyrdom (lines 1-65), her ecstatic vision (lines 65-121), and her apotheosis (lines 121-182). While the entire poem unmistakably takes on hues of the *Vida* and other works by Teresa, in scattered hints and details, the first two parts draw very directly on the first and twenty-ninth chapters of the *Vida*, and the apotheosis, somewhat different from them, is fashioned mainly out of Crashaw's own imagination. As one reads the poem (which is printed here as Part III) the three phases move as one long drift of meaning: a symbolic journey to glory. It is not the movement of an ordinary life, from morn to climatic noon into evening, but of a transcending life which progresses uncertainly from morn through midday up to the triumphant moment when the would-be night becomes the dawn of eternity.

An author, we may remember, is an *auctor*, an augmenter. Ortega y Gasset's model poet aggrandizes the world by adding to the raw substance the continents of his own imagination. The poet who goes beyond the aim of giving beauty and order to experience may increase his reader's sense of the wholeness of being, of 'total reality.' Within the scope of a few pages Crashaw concentrates total reality in Teresa. He aggrandizes, but not choosing to add new continents of his own, he imaginatively transforms her language, character, and atmosphere into a poem. The effect of its unusually full development is not close definition and completeness. Instead one slowly penetrates through layers of events, motives, and emotions, to the saint's inner nature. From this point of view chronology, sequence, and individual history are no more than the superficies of the subject, and the *Vida*, the chapel, and the poem may all be 'read' in the same way. All three acknowledge time as an external mode of order which is to be denied or destroyed. The processes are not simple, however, and though Teresa's work is less symbolic than Bernini's or Crashaw's all three reflect the complications of human experience. Where Crashaw and Bernini are concerned, many resemblances originate in the *Vida* itself, but there are others too.

As well as the *concetto* of fire, the phenomenon of movement is in both— more comprehensive and manifold than fire, which is one form of movement, but not more central. And differences soon appear too, some of them attributable to difference in medium. Though the progress of both works is by upward steps: earth, ecstasy, eternity, the chapel has four levels, and the poem three: the poem's lowest level, where love and death compete for mastery, is a fair equivalent to the levels of death and life which comprise the Order of Nature in the chapel. In addition the poem's dramatic emphasis is not on ecstasy but ecstasy and apotheosis together. However, regardless of the different emphasis, the full scope and culmination of the two is the same. It is the same Teresa, ageless, intense, and silent. In the poem her thoughts never become speech, and in the sculpture her mouth is shaped only for inaudible moans. As Bernini's saint is placed in a scene suggestive of her spiritual ascent after death, Crashaw's is carried along on the rhythms of what she will become.

Three

Love's Descent

The brief introduction to the Hymn refers in toneless words to Teresa as a child endowed with 'masculine courage' who 'outran maturity.' If for one deceptive moment we imagine her as a simple, saintly little girl, the opening lines dispel the idea. At the summoning of the poet, Love invisibly descends –

> Love, thou art absolute sole lord
> of life and death . . .

– and as Crashaw's rhetoric of the sublime takes hold of the lines it becomes clear that Love's presence in Teresa makes childlike simplicity impossible.

Love, as the principal name for Christ, is the under-theme of the whole poem. It generates its energy and determines its direction, especially in the first thirty-five lines where it is nine times placed prominently at or near the front of the lines. In a swelling tide Love will flood over Teresa and the unearthly poetic landscape. The reader's consciousness is filled by the word, even though it reappears afterwards at only a few scattered points.

In the poem's opening phase (to line 65) Love is declared to be the 'word' the poem aims 'to prove' – and the connotation of the verb is not only *to test* but *to know by experience,* exactly in the manner of other Metaphysical poems and Bernini's chapel. The word will be proved by appealing *not* to 'old soldiers' of martyrdom and *not* to those whose 'spacious bosoms spread a throne' for the love of Christ to occupy, but to Love in the 'soul of a soft child.' The main meaning of the opening paragraph describes a wide, downward curve which starts at the summons to Love, swings out toward the two familiar but inapplicable kinds of martyr, and stops at Teresa the child. The solemn force of the various kinds of *o* in 'Love . . . abs*o*lute s*o*le l*o*rd' spreads, with a dozen lines of strong, straying sounds, before settling down into mildness with the fluent sounds of *m*, *l*, and *s*

> . . . *s*ee hi*m* take a private *s*eat,
> *M*aking his *m*ansion in the *mil*d
> And *mil*ky *soul* of a *s*oft chi*l*d.

Henceforth the focus of the poem stays fixed on Teresa. Before the descent of Love she has no existence whatever. Afterwards, she exists and her awareness grows, though falteringly at first. As yet, Love is not recognized as either the divine destroyer or her 'sov'reign spouse.' The poem develops a number of questions and paradoxes which in time become resolved. 'What death with Love should have to do' Teresa does not know, but will know. What she seeks will not come, and what she does not seek will come. Whether she is living to die or dying to live, the unchanging presence is Love.

When Love descends and inhabits Teresa's soul her reaction is a self-abandoning desire for death. The 'masculine courage' which associated her with the 'old soldiers' of martyrdom enables her even at six to face the worst fears 'man trembles at.' Very deliberately Crashaw sets her off against the active martyrs as a completely passive and expectant recipient of Love. The throne made ready, and the soldiers loudly defying death and reaching for martyr-crowns of glory, are the antithesis of the soft child. In forging her new nature out of contradictory qualities, Crashaw makes her both like and unlike these soldiers. The zealous strain of 'blood and sweat' like theirs contrasts with the soft soul where Love comes to live, as the size of the soldiers 'great and tall,' or with 'spacious bosoms,' does with the small child. Magnitude is first refuted, then restored in a new form: when Divine Love builds a *mansion* in the soul of a child, it must enlarge it and change it, for Love has dominion over life and death. Throughout the poem Christ as Love holds sway over Teresa, under the various names of the Word, the Lamb, the Spouse, the King, the Lord.[104]

'Scarce hath she learned to lisp the name of martyr,' than she is ready to buy a brave death with her life. 'Scarce hath she blood enough' to make a sword-blade blush with guilt, says the inverted hyperbole.

And for the time being the lines float close to the ground, energetic but unclear in direction. Here Teresa, though guidance and grace are available to her, moves about in the Order of Nature, only later to become part of the Order of Grace. Even in this earthly zone where the phenomenal world could look normal, the scene and atmosphere are strangely unreal. We are again in the factually blank world of the *Vida*. Nothing has form or feature. Because everything in the poem aspires to the spiritual state, Crashaw's outward vision is dim. Objects, when they exist, are insubstantial and colourless. The hints of colour which occur, all late in the poem, are less colours than spiritual qualities: the white moon, the white steps, the rosy love of Christ. The situation is clear, but the place and action are even less clear than in the *Vida*. Here Teresa's mother and father appear not as people but parts of people: the father's 'knee,' the mother's 'arms' and 'kisses' – no more. Teresa herself has no visible appearance, no physical environment. The poem can do what a statue or painting cannot: Teresa exists here without an appearance, yet the subtlest changes in her states of mind and awareness, are expressed lightly, and often subliminally. It is as if life on earth were a sea-dream where everything is indistinct and weightless, wafted along by unremitting currents. As for a time in the *Vida*, her will is alive and active, but not in control.

There comes to the surface only one historical event from Teresa's life, the same which always finds a place in the biographies and legend of Teresa. It is her early attempt to be martyred by the Moors. We recall that the *Vida* deals very briefly with the event. After reading saints' lives and playing games as hermits in the orchard at home, Teresa and her brother Rodrigo were fired with the desire to die like saints,

> not out of any love for God of which I was conscious, but in order to attain as quickly as possible to the fruition of the great blessings which, as I read, were laid up in heaven.

So they agreed to go to the Moors by begging their bread on the way. They left, and would have gone ahead but for one difficulty: 'our greatest hindrance seemed to be that we had a father and a mother.' The early biographers Ribera and Yepes add to this that the two left home by way of the Adaja bridge where they were found by an uncle who brought them back to their terrified mother. Under sharp reprimand Rodrigo unchivalrously put all the blame on *la niña Teresa*.[105]

The only *fact* given in the poem is that the girl of six leaves home to seek martyrdom, but Crashaw wraps the event in layers of ignorance, compulsion, and mystery. She has no idea what love has to do with death, nor why she must die a martyr. In Teresa's failure to explain love we see the very things it is not, namely intellect, maturity, and physical strength. It is her heart, touched by Love, which dares prove that love is stronger than death. She must seek what she cannot find in the loving arms of her family:

> Since 'tis not to be had at home
> She'll travel for a martyrdom.
> No home for her confesses she
> But where she may a martyr be.

Her active inaction at this point has the quivering quality of uncertain energy. 'Though she cannot tell you why, she can love and she can die' still denies one other truth about martyrdom. Like ecstasy in the *Vida*, like love itself in this poem, martyrdom cannot be willed. Since desire may be egotism rather than a loving surrender of the will, she can only prepare for it. The rest is up to God.

Yet the remoteness of her union with God does not remove the desire for fulfilment, it accentuates it. Each impulse of energy is a yearning in that direction. No wonder Teresa cannot fathom the connection between love and death (which in the opening phase of the poem is three times compressed into single lines). She does not see that her fulfilment will be a love-death. The Mystical Marriage of Teresa and her 'fair spouse' is a melody developed by the subtle entwining of birth, joy, fruition, wounding, sighing, love, and death. Perhaps Simone Weil is right: one must not reproach the mystics for using love's language. 'It is theirs by right. Others only borrow it.'[106]

The idea of 'plenitude' met with so often in seventeenth-century literature and seen so often in the art, here points to fulfilment in divine union. The life of the poem is fulfilment and fruition, a theme Crashaw elaborates with various forms of *fruit*, *fill*, and *full*. In the Thomistic sense, if perfection is full, and human evil or imperfection is a falling away from the fullness of perfection, then the poem seeks to regain this fullness. The desire of the martyrs Crashaw mentions is to have love *fill* their throne; midway in the poem the promise for Teresa is 'full joys.' At the start it is 'fruitless wishes' which drive her from home, and at the conclusion her soul is 'made fruitful.' The distinction Teresa at first fails to make is between winning fruit for herself and pursuing Divine Love selflessly. At this time, in fact, she imagines she is possessed by the love which does not yet possess her.

The lines of this opening section press urgently forward to glory right now. The impatience is checked only a little as the momentum is built up by a group of thematic words, not only *love* and *death*, but *blood*, *heart*, and *fire*. The five together already begin to compose the saint's story. The theme of sacrificial blood is soon played out, and thereafter the word is not repeated again. Just once and very quickly, the connection is made between Christ's blood and Teresa's: she shall 'leave amongst them sown her Lord's blood, or at least her own.' The themes of *heart* and *fire*, on the other hand, have only begun to appear. These large monosyllabic words are so important that they determine the poem's rise and fall. After the opening plunge the movement is tentative but quite steady to the end of the third verse paragraph, at which point the energy of Teresa's divine passion suddenly breaks loose.

> Love touched her heart, and lo it beats
> High, and burns with such brave heats,
> Such thirsts to die, as dares drink up
> A thousand cold deaths in one cup.
> Good reason, for she breathes all fire.
> Her weak breast heaves with strong desire. . . .

The sensuous pressure of the heat, thirst, fire, and desire working against her heart, creates new lyrical force. That exclamatory peak is the highest in this opening movement, and the section on martyrdom which comes after it moves with almost as much force. In this relatively earth-bound part of the poem there appears all at once a commercial metaphor which seems to keep the movement low and horizontal. 'She'll to the Moors and trade with them' we are told, and 'she'll offer them her dearest breath . . . in change for death. She'll bargain with them. . . .' Perhaps there is irony in this. In such a transaction, life and death are not things to be traded but freely given and received. So the speculative account of the martyrdom ends wasted, its energy running down in the series of 'Farewells.'

In the poem as a whole the spiritual energy does not run down, it increases. There are fluctuations, there is restraint and delay, but Crashaw keeps the flow of energy continuous, mainly by means of the words he chooses and the way he forms those words into rhymed couplets. At least on the surface, the simplicity of the poetry can be seen and felt as readily as the contours of Bernini's statue. Less easily understood, however, is the rhythm of the poetic lines. Perhaps the rhythm of poetry, like rhythm in music, gains its great significance by paralleling or simulating the intrinsic rhythms of life – the cadences of the day, the season, the life-span, and the cadences of the body walking, dancing, working, and living by pulse and heartbeat. The basic beat is held, but like reality itself, the rhythm of poetry is not perfectly regular. In all but the simplest forms, poetry works best when the poet knows exactly when and how to interrupt or vary the rhythm. Without the variations, Crashaw's metre would beat like a metronome and Bernini's rhythmically carved surfaces would look like corrugation.

The smallest and steadiest rhythmic element is the throb of the iambics. By the time he wrote this ode Crashaw's rhythms had become freer and more varied. The size of the units increases nicely: the iambics combine into lines, the lines into couplets, and the couplets into verse paragraphs. His essential line is a short one of eight beats. Momentum is held by that basic beat. On the other hand the unusually fluent quality of the verse carries the motion forward. Half the lines run on from one verse to the next. Especially at one highly excited interval the lines are a beat or two shorter than normal and the motion drives ahead even faster. The momentum is held by other means too. For example, the poem's future-leaning purpose is expressed mainly by present and future verbs, and by a scattering of imperatives and subjunctives (here the potential mode) which do nothing to interfere with the effect. At the same time, the motion is also retarded. The strong rhyming of the couplets slows the pace, and the choppy phrasing and breaking of both rhythm and rhyme restrain it. Rhyming is broken only twice (at lines 100 and 120) but rhythm constantly is, because the metrical accent comes anywhere along the lines. Imperceptibly the authority of metre and rhythm controls Teresa's fervour, but the irregularities and changes in pace also release it. Later, in her rapture, she becomes ecstatically agitated like the sculpture, and the verse reflects that, or creates the agitation, as it does in the final part after Teresa's translation to the celestial level, when a fairly regular beat is resumed. But until that time both the forward thrust of the rhythm and its restraint belong to her inner state. Together they develop a pulsating tension between her progress and the errors and obstacles impeding it. The poet makes us aware of Teresa's tension as she is not. All she is now aware of is the impatient desire to die immediately.

And the wording contributes much to this. Crashaw's slim, spare language is built up out of an extraordinarily small stock of very common words. One comes to see how much advantage is in that quality of commonness. The words yoke the familiar and particular to the universal, and the repetition of their sounds, as we shall see, saturates us with their meaning. Here the two principles of first importance are that the main elements are nearly all monosyllabic, remarkably monosyllabic, and that they are repeated. It bears some resemblance to Racine's spare, simple-looking style which repeats key words, like *fureur* and *feu* in *Phèdre*, with powerful rhetorical effect. But Crashaw's style is different, and his rhetoric is different. The French of Racine's day lacked the flexibility of English. Consequently Crashaw is always alert to what can be gained by slightly varying both the forms and arrangement of words. The rhythms of many repeated sounds pour meanings and half-meanings over one another, not only making the primary meaning penetrate more deeply but creating an ambiance for it. On their own account sounds (which are never sense by themselves) develop an extra dimension of sense. What are mere trifles do, in the aggregate, increase celestiality, or tension, or, at this point, the depth and urgency of Teresa's love which '*kn*ows *no non*age, *nor* the mind,' '*b*eats *high*, and *burns* with such *brave heats*, such th*irsts* to *die*.'

From the moment her heart is set aflame by love, and it beats, burns, and thirsts for death, the Teresan language turns richly extravagant – a strangely sub-sensuous and super-sensuous expression which now begins to become incantation. Some readers may find the rhetoric perfectly tuned to her psychic state; others who cannot or will not grasp it, may dismiss it as merely excessive. In Mario Praz's opinion that Crashaw is overwhelmed by a world of images he cannot control, only the word 'cannot' is questionable.[107] In the attempt to reach beyond the margins of known experience, he deliberately will not keep the overwhelming images in control. The point about Teresa's language here is not control but yielding. She is reckless, ardent, over the edge and boldly daring. As in the *Vida*, her wilfulness is extreme but rather brief. Ortega y Gasset's version of Teresa would be that her destiny is not determined by choice but by some hidden current of energy, some internal force which totally overpowers her and could easily destroy her. As in the *Vida* the soul in the lower degrees of prayer was separating itself from earthly and selfish things, it does so here. But because Teresa of the *Vida* sees herself in the past, retrospectively, while Crashaw imagines her between now and the future, the poem is more inconsistent and baffling. She is one who loves though incapable of loving, one who has 'angelical' knowledge though an unknowing child. Henceforth her personal will is surrendered to the divine will. In the language of the *Vida*, the will now working within her is not her own. Coming to know the ways of Love she shall soon know the submissiveness of Bernini's Teresa.

Crashaw creates a transitional world which has much, but not everything, in common with Bernini's. The present Teresa is not exactly the Teresa who will be – *change* is exhibitable, various moods and motives are exhibitable, ambiguities are, and so are areas of consciousness which, through the skill of the poet, either join Teresa to God, the poet, or the reader, or disjoin her from them. An essential distinction is that Bernini's statue, visually speaking, must project her all at once and irrecoverably, while Crashaw can show a continuous image, or a multiplication of images, fixed in sequence and controlled in time. But each medium has its price to pay, and though Crashaw can express memory, touches of irony, and changes in his attitude toward Teresa as he traces out her spiritual life, he can in fact show nothing of the brilliant immediacy of Teresa's presence in marble.

Crashaw enters the saint's experience, or keeps it remote, shifting his distance and angle of vision as the occasion requires. At first he stands conspicuously over the scene, watching, reporting, commenting, explaining. Teresa is scarcely visible *except* through him. Imaginatively speaking, Crashaw several times changes his spatial relation to her. Since he stays anonymous it is not important that he is present in the work, as Bernini never is, but it is very important that his role of speaker permits him these changes in attitude and tone. Teresa's childhood is being judged by him, but soon he becomes less her judge and more her eager and sympathetic adviser, expressing her intentions as though they belong to a future which he knows and she does not: 'Farewell then, all the world! Adieu! Teresa is no more for you.' The tone Crashaw adopts for her farewell from home is touched with sentimental mock-heroism: the Moorish expedition is foolishly mistaken. Then very quickly, in the second phase, the tone changes to almost paternal sympathy, with 'Sweet, not so fast!' She is then regarded with affectionate condescension. It is only a passing flicker of meaning, but different from any refinement in Bernini. In bringing this inspired 'child' toward eternal fulfilment Crashaw pictures her leaving home for a marriage consummated in Christ. The word 'spouse' occurring at four widely separated intervals in the poem keeps us aware of what may be called the dramatic pattern of the total. It is the familiar theme of the nun going to her marriage with Christ, but like all experience in the poem the narrative is deeply internalized. As Teresa quits the role of loving child to become the lover of Christ, the poetry rises and the poet's perspective changes. Though present, he never speaks as 'I' nor reveals himself autobiographically like Montaigne or Thomas Browne. We seem not to see him because he is always facing toward Teresa, not us, and we are onlookers or overhearers.

Four

The Ecstatic Environment

An ingenious theory mentioned by Roger Fry turns on the idea that Spanish art has value only when we do not look at it. It exists to induce particular states of mind, to bring forth a response of wonder, awe, and mystery. In less extreme terms this means that *behind* Spanish religious art, which is religious to a degree no other art of Europe is religious, there is something primary going on. The superfluity and confusion of the gold and glitter in the semi-darkness of a church can by itself make a viewer feel exalted and spell-bound. What is seen is less important than what is felt within, however. The mode of Crashaw's art, its impressive rather than expressive character, the hazy quality of high states of excitement, the ritual imagery, all put him in touch with Fry's theory: 'The architecture, the sculpture and painting in a Spanish church are all accessory to the purely dramatic art – the religious dance, if you like – of the Mass.'[108]

The melting form of Teresa placed over an altar depicting the Last Supper brings out just such suggestions in Bernini's chapel. Crashaw's poem – more exactly its middle section – is nothing less than a communion movement. The impression develops gradually, as if one design were showing through another. The drama of the Mystical Marriage sketched in over the whole surface of the poem does not conflict with this design but actually provides the situation for it. Details describing the ecstatic transport also describe, subordinately, the experience of a High Mass: the soul's readiness, the 'still-surviving funeral,' the 'lump of incense,' the 'perfuming clouds,' the exhalation to heaven.

This second phase of the poem (lines 65 to about 121) is the ecstatic death which brings the saint into the Order of Grace. If death itself is but an instant, this cannot be death. The event will be a climax, to be sure, but a climax which is prolonged like the ecstasy of the statue, prolonged on almost the same level for the remainder of the poem. The ecstasy itself does not occur in one, two, or three lines but almost forty, first as Love's dart inflicts the wounds through his seraphic agents, and then, after a lyrical cry of bliss, a second time, with Teresa explicitly reacting to the wounds before swiftly exhaling to heaven as a lump of incense wasted by fire.[109]

Accustomed as we may be to the planned spontaneity of baroque works there is something unexpected in the gentle, swift command which calls Teresa back from her Moorish expedition: 'Sweet, not so fast!' Of course it is Christ the 'fair spouse' who calls her back and bids her 't'embrace a milder martyrdom.' A death it shall be, but 'a death more mystical and high.' Coming at almost the halfway point in the poem, that phrase defines everything that follows. In those lines, free and buoyant but very highly concentrated by comparison with the two hundred pages of the *Vida* devoted to it, the girl of six, anxious to bleed on a 'barb'rous knife,' is converted into a woman dying a mystical death.

A radical change in the poet's relationship to Teresa increases and complicates his involvement. Up to now Teresa has been addressed as 'she,' but from this point forward she becomes 'thou.' The spectacle of divinity filled Crashaw with awe and amazement. Like Bernini he enters the saint's experience as if revealing it from the inside. Yet the intimacy suggested by the second-person is a little misleading. 'Thee' and 'thou' could conceivably open up a dialogue, but they never do. In addition, the sense of intimacy is reduced by the hypothetical nature of the event. We remind ourselves that the whole sweep of her history is imagined into the future. Nevertheless, for Crashaw and for us the time of maximum involvement in the poem is during this interval of ecstasy. After that the distance between us and her, spatially and spiritually, is variable, until it eventually becomes vague and indefinable. At certain moments she appears to be simultaneously close and distant, just as Bernini's Teresa is irresistibly inviting yet not easy to approach. And at one point when Crashaw himself is half-transported into glory with her, he still beholds Teresa in heaven 'there,' from his place on earth 'here,' like some enraptured figure of El Greco or Zurbarán with eyes upturned. In fact the evolution of Crashaw's attitudes toward Teresa is determined by her changes from childhood to martyrdom and from martyrdom to glory.

At this point the lines shake off their earthly bonds. Turned away earlier by 'Sweet, not so fast!', the saint is now carried swiftly by the exuberance of 'fast shalt thou exhale to heav'n.' Having discovered that 'love is eloquence' Crashaw discharges the long climax in scattered, quivering phrases of truthful absurdity. One cannot even locate the centre of the climax, perhaps because the outward form of it anticipates by only a pulse-beat the spiritual form of it within, as sometimes happens in Rembrandt, and Bernini. The rise begins from the moment the knife becomes the dart, not held by one seraph but a throng of seraphim who descend as 'love's soldiers.' The cry of painful bliss is an extraordinary burst of staccato lines whose pressure is the greater for their being held in and cut short – until the normal sixth and seventh lines open into the eighth which is let out to inordinate length as it plays on the paradox of life and death. What the lines actually do is register the *effects* of the dart wounds in a string of impassioned, semi-articulate utterances, a series of contradictory ejaculations breaking up on the edge of reason and understanding.

> O how oft shalt thou complain
> Of a sweet and subtle pain!
> Of intolerable joys!
> Of a death in which who dies
> Loves his death, and dies again,
> And would forever so be slain!
> And lives and dies and knows not why
> To live, but that he thus may never leave to die.

Living, loving, dying, expressed many times before, are many times refined by each other, accumulated and compressed so as to give multiplicity the impression of singleness and permanence. The bitter-sweet rapture, the mingling of acute agitation and serene peace, the poignancy of what can be grasped only insecurely – all this is held lightly in the tensions of 'sweet and subtle pain,' 'intolerable joys,' and 'delicious wounds' which come with the death of one who loves death and 'would forever so be slain.'

It is this paradox of ecstasy which again catches Teresa's ambiguous condition, a revival of the *molesta suavitas* or *suavis molestia* which frequent the writing of St Bernard and St Francis, and continue to appear in St Teresa and St John of the Cross. Exuberance of phrasing does something for the ineffable, but not enough. There is the need for figurative language like this paradox and for what Teresa calls 'holy absurdities' – those strange assertions, like *life* bleeding on a knife, like a *funeral* falling into Love's arms, which are irrational but understandable. The emancipating effect of this 'logic of spirit' increases as the poem advances, as though deepening the soul's potential for freedom by gradually rejecting matter and its laws.

In the opinion of Maritain poetry, as something more than verse-making, is 'a process both more general and more primary' than art. Identifying poetry's greater abstraction with its capacity to approach ultimate meanings, he believes it to be 'that inter-communication between the inner being of things and inner being of the human Self which is a kind of divination' – a divination which summons up shades of the Latin *vates* and Plato's μουσικός.[110] At the least one may say that poetry like Crashaw's can create a spiritual atmosphere which is rarer than things seen visually, rare like the atmosphere of music.

The subconscious effects of sound and rhythm build up meanwhile. Crashaw's 'musical' use of sound (and we may remind ourselves that this is a hymn) makes meaning advance or fold back on itself through delicately elaborate repetition and variation. In simple instances one sound holds a group of lines together.

> *F*it executioners *f*or thee,
> The *f*air'st and *f*irst-born sons of *f*ire,
> Blest sera*ph*im. . . .

Sometimes sounds played into the ear subside for a while and then recur, as when 'she's for the *M*oors and *m*artyrdom' goes underground for twenty-five lines before coming up again and attaching to 'th'i*mm*ortal instru*m*ent.' Or sounds may group hard together in intricate involutions, like the five sounds in one couplet:

> A *d*art thrice *d*ippe*d* in that *r*ich flame
> Which *wr*ites thy spouse's *r*a*d*iant name.

Readers hear with different ears, of course, and numerous patterns of sound are interwoven. A light sweep over many strings which joins sound to meaning, sometimes plays out whole themes in the poem. In one very prominent instance a group of sounds traces the awakening of Teresa's understanding of what she is doing and where she is going: the liquid fluency of *m* (and *n*), *l*, and *r*. When first she childishly longed for death and had scarcely '*l*earned to *l*isp the *n*ame of *m*artyr,' she was not aware that '*l*ove, *n*ot years *n*or *l*imbs . . . can *m*ake the *m*artyr or the *m*an.' In seeking a 'ho*m*e' not 'a*m*ongst her *m*other's kisses' but 'where she *m*ay a *m*artyr be,' she is carried along by a gentle roll of like sounds, from the '*M*oors and *m*artyrdom' to the '*m*i*l*der *m*artyrdom' which anticipates, quite beyond her awareness, 'i*mm*orta*l* we*l*comes,' 's*mil*es of heav'*n*,' and her marriage with 'the *L*a*m*b, thy *L*ord.'

This particular theme of sounds may seem to dominate the poem, yet parallel themes have equal importance in the polyphonous form. Still another theme, of mainly monosyllabic words, strengthens the existential qualities of her mystical history. The death-theme crosses the love-theme with the harsh Anglo-Saxon sounds of *die, death,* and *dart* adding to the threat of violence and loss. *Die* and *death* first subdue and extinguish the kindred sounds of *breath, buy, deny,* and *breast,* which denote life on earth. By dying to love Teresa makes *die* and *death* lose their terrestrial meaning. They are replaced by *life* and *live* for the rest of the poem, and it is the ecstasy which makes the change. Teresa will die again and again until, mysteriously, all the deaths will become one death – which is no death but the dying from life into Life. At the same time other words, *crown, joys, heart, name,* and indeed *fire* and *martyrdom,* which come early in the poem, all emerge again in new forms. Each undergoes change of meaning, is born again like a phoenix out of the ashes – a bird much favoured among Teresa's metaphors. In a similar way the sound of *die* is also reborn into the new sounds and meanings of *sigh, high, smile, delight, bright, white,* and *light.* And ultimately the long *i* sound of *die* gives way also to the transcendent word *life* and the word above all words, *Christ.*

The key words seem to move freely about, colliding and connecting with each other in their flight. Sounds establish contact with like sounds so that while *breath* links with *death* it also rises to join *bright,* which adheres to *light,* as *light* does to *life,* and *life* to *love.* Not one esoteric word or phrase appears in the poem. Always the wording is extremely selective, and the range of sounds narrow and very exact in effect. Whatever Eliot had in mind when suggesting a likeness between Crashaw's poetry and the interior of St Peter's, it could not have been this homogeneity. Whether bunched together or scattered out, like sounds attract each other and the associations yield new meaning. In the end the mounting effect of all these recurrent sounds is a semi-reality between consciousness and oblivion, the aura of peaceful excitement which is being formed around the moment of ecstasy.

The poem as a whole produces the same sense of movement and rising as Bernini's chapel. The essence of it is the rhythms in both. Theorists write that rhythm in literature and music corresponds to pattern in the visual arts, and the idea sounds persuasive. But often the correspondence is less useful and dependable than it seems, particularly for works like these in which both time and space have strongly metaphorical functions that permit them to break away from their individual media and approach each other. 'Rhythm relates to movement, as movement relates to change,' says Ernest Mundt, as though speaking directly to the idea of *change* in works, and in a related statement, 'rhythm suggests form as it applies to motion,' reminds us of what we need to know about these non-static forms.[111] The forms involve motion. As soon as we hold them stark still, they are falsified. It is therefore essential to see the kinds of movement shared by the chapel and poem. Aside from the content itself (which is no small matter), the resemblances between these works, including movement, are all metaphorical and symbolic. Of course the principal ones reside in the two presentations of Teresa herself, but others extend well beyond, into the far corners of the works.

We recall the many means Bernini used to create movement in the Cornaro Chapel. The appearance and arrangement of the marbles is in itself a fantastic flurry of motions – the fluidness of the *africano* in the main columns, the mottled vibrancy of the *verde antico* pilasters, the wavy, spreading patterns of the onyx panels on the walls beside Teresa, are only the most prominent (PLATES V and IX, and FRONTISPIECE). There is also a suggestion of movement in the vertical arrangement of the columns and pilasters themselves, and much more in the spacing of the architectural bands, mouldings, and borders, and in the intricate rhythms of the decorative motifs: garlands, egg-and-dart design, series of swirls, leafy brackets alternating with carved roses, strings of angels placed fairly regularly on the front curve of the vault, and the heavy relief border running around the chapel at the top of the architectural frame (PLATES V, XIX, and XX). These and other features which stimulate the sense of motion – including of course the relatively consistent rhythm of the folds and hollows of Teresa's robes and the rising flame-lines of the seraph's garment – flatly contradict the static qualities of the chapel. And within this complex of movements is the instinct to rise, the tendency for clouds, wings, upward-thrusting columns and pediment, and the vertical plan of the chapel to carry us upward either by steep vertical steps or through free space.

The poem's forward movement is also a rising, even though it comes as a surprise that Crashaw never once uses an explicit word for rising, and suggests the idea at one point only with 'exhale to heav'n.' Instead Crashaw's figure of Teresa merely appears on the higher level of ecstasy, as though placed there like Bernini's figure. It is the hovering presence of Divine Love which makes her seem to float as if on the point of rising. And since her body, described only as separate features, never has coherence and weight, it gives the impression of freedom, and the freedom to rise. Teresa in words and Teresa in marble are kept equally light.

Crashaw's rhythms and movement are above all a matter of *feeling*. Speaking in a low key the historical St Teresa had said, 'What I seek to explain is the feelings of the soul when it is in this divine union.' Teresa's ecstasy and death are mysteries in Crashaw, and the transformation to follow is a greater mystery still. To express it fully in poetry is beyond anyone's capacity. 'Ask not the tongues of men.' The illusionism, the simulation of these high states of being by means of figurative language, is Crashaw's only resort. 'Suffice thy self shall *feel* thine own full joys,' he says, speaking for the reader as well. The word *feeling* has lost caste nowadays, and what we distrust about it is the very indefiniteness which Crashaw and St Teresa freely exploit. Crashaw knew what Dante knew before him and Yeats after him, that rhythm creates and prolongs a mood of contemplation, that it works by its power of incantation. Stripped of these qualities, dart, wound, heart, and fire are no more than words of fact.

Five

Teresa's Wound of Love

Teresa almost goes to meet the instrument of her ecstatic death:

> How kindly will thy gentle heart
> Kiss the sweetly-killing dart!

The wound in the heart – those words or that picture – while never so popular in England, is one of Crashaw's strongest links with the Baroque on the continent. Like Teresa herself he is among the imagistic rather than philosophic interpreters of mystical experience.[112] He may never have seen Murillo, Gaulli, Lanfranco, or any of the painters he resembles, but he would surely have had to see emblem books in England or abroad. The Christianizing process had been going on for a long span of centuries. Christian churches were erected on pagan temple sites, Christian holy days were superimposed on old feast days, Augustine replaced Ovid, and Minerva became the Blessed Virgin.[113] Between St Teresa's death and Crashaw's birth the collections of de Montenay and Vaenius also changed emblem books from profane to sacred. Cupid yields his bow and arrows to become the Infant Jesus, the Angel of the Annunciation, or, as in the present case, Christ's angel of love. Scores of times the allegorical war of love is presented as an arrangement of arrows, flames, and wings around their vital centre, the heart. In George Wither's collection true love appears as a flaming heart clasped by two hands and surmounted by a death's head. In numerous ingenious narratives the heart is chief character; Anton Wiericx made prints not only of Teresa in the seraphic ecstasy but of the heart as a stage on which was shown a long allegory of Christ's life and death. Or the heart is the house of Christ as in Henry Hawkins' *The Devout Heart* (1634) and in Crashaw's poem a dozen years after. Baroque Europe saw many versions of this drama revived as the 'cult of the heart' or the 'cult of the Infant Jesus.'[114]

That many English writers made extensive use of emblem books has already been remarked. It is George Herbert one thinks of first. In writing 'Good Friday' he is believed to have had emblems of the heart specifically in mind.[115] Herbert did not produce or use actual emblems, but faint signs of them remain in the background, and not uncommonly emblems must have been the pictorial stimulus for entirely new poems. With Crashaw the case is nothing so clear. We know he did engravings for *Carmen Deo Nostro*. We know he had the habit of picture-thinking. And we can assume he was influenced by emblem books – and particularly here where he is presenting to us the poem's central image of Teresa in ecstasy. Crashaw might have seen heart emblems in a number of places, in Hawkins or another book, or in the concordance made at Little Gidding by Nicholas Ferrar.[116] Whatever he saw, his picture-thinking may have been a factor in making Teresa's ecstasy a 'milder martyrdom' in which no blood flows and no raw flesh is seen.

This is the absolute moment of change, yet Bernini and Crashaw present the event completely without violence. For both, the significance of the wounding is internal. It is the *effect* of the event on Teresa which is primary, just as in Milton's 'Nativity Ode' and Tintoretto's *Entombment* it is the effect of Christ's Birth and death on mankind which is expressed. Although Crashaw's lines keep the saint at a respectful distance and may lack some of the personalness of the historical Teresa's phenomenal paroxysm, they have the authentic intensity of her autobiographical account of the dart penetrating deeply, many times, with a pain 'so sharp that it made me utter several moans; so excessive was the sweetness caused by this intense pain that one can never wish to lose it.'

The paramount characteristic of this 'death' is its utter gentleness. The smile of Bernini's seraph, almost the archetype of beatific smiles, bathes Teresa in gentleness[117] (PLATES II and XXIII). His whole form is gentle – the delicate lines of his arms, wrists, and hands, the smoothly rounded contours of his muscles, the unbellicose bend of his neck. The wounds of the poem are welcomed, needed, health-giving, and because they weep balsam which salves them, also self-healing. As the *charitatis victima* Teresa is neither pierced nor burned by the flaming dart. Her reaction to the wounds is 'kindly,' and the dart itself, an immortal instrument which is 'spiritual, pure, and fair,' completes the conception of gentleness.

In neither work can the wounds be seen. As the original St Teresa desired 'only to hug my pain,' Crashaw's wants to close the wound in her embraces. At no point in the poem is there closer physical contact. Here if anywhere one would expect the dart to enter her body. But like the 'barb'rous knife' of the Moors, it does not penetrate; the first was an abortive attempt to die; the second a 'milder martyrdom.' We might now expect to 'see' Teresa with a vividness comparable to her sculptured form. But we do not. Teresa is all metaphors, oblique glimpses, and atmosphere. She consists of scattered elements – breath, heart, wounds, kisses, a dying sigh, and no more. She is sensed almost super-sensuously, acted upon and reacting. As was noted, *blood* in Crashaw's ode is a mundane word confined to the early part. Here in the climax the death-dart does not cut her flesh but *tastes* her *breath*. Incongruously active yet submissive she *kisses* the dart, yet kisses it not with her lips but her *heart*, the vital centre of her love.

After the wounding, after the incredible dart is dipped in Teresa's fire and writes the name of Christ across the sky, the tension of the poem increases further. In rapture 'we must risk everything,' says Teresa. The fulfilment is now to come 'fast'. That is Crashaw's word and Teresa's inclination. Driven by spiritual passion the lines move with easy rapidity, swift, poised, and buoyant.

> When these thy deaths so numerous,
> Shall all at last die into one,
> And melt thy soul's sweet mansion,
> Like a soft lump of incense, hasted
> By too hot a fire, and wasted
> Into perfuming clouds, so fast
> Shalt thou exhale to heav'n at last
> In a resolving sigh. . . .

The 'death more mystical and high' is not on the Erasmian model of the soul's severance from the body, of spirit from flesh, or of God from the mind. 'Thy deaths so numerous' are the 'daily dying' understood by most men of Crashaw's era – death as part of the life-cycle experienced many, many times within this life. When death itself comes, it is not a terminus but a passing phase which completes the actual cycle of a life. It is a transition 'while one is yet alive' (St Bernard), a transition in which one 'lives while yet dying' (St John of the Cross). In another poem Crashaw holds the concept in perfect focus: 'this loving strife of living death and dying life.'

Bernini's illusionistic presentation of Teresa depends mainly on his manner of carving her face, limbs, and robes; Crashaw's on paradox, metaphor, and the language of elation. Both required an equivalent for what the literature of mysticism calls 'the spiritual incision,' and this they found in the *concetto* of fire – fire as the energy, ardour, and motion of Divine Love, as the substantial-insubstantial element in nature, and in the poem, as the constant which defines Teresa as child, martyr, and saint. Between the two works it is the sharpest, most subtle, most inward resemblance of all, the one in which other resemblances meet.

The leap is effortless from the child who 'breathes all fire' and 'burns with such brave heats' to the woman dying to love by the flaming dart held by the 'fair'st and first-born sons of fire.' The imprint of the *Vida* is freshly stamped on the verses: the seraph's face was 'so aflame that he appeared to be one of the highest types of angel who seem to be all afire.' At the tip of his golden dart Teresa apparently saw 'a point of fire' (*un poco de fuego*). The resemblance to Bernini's saint and seraph calls for no more elaboration: the posture and surface of the melting saint, the flamy gathering of cloth at her neck, and the flambant seraph whose torso makes a billow of fire which in small wisps reaches his hair and wings.

The 'sweetly-killing dart' of the poetry changes Teresa into celestial form as if by the magic touch of a wand. Her death is not an incineration but an 'exhalation.' Death neither maims nor destroys her but *melts* her like a lump of incense. At the decisive moment of Teresa's change, transformation by melting is an astonishing death, yet more astonishing in our day then Crashaw's. It was written by Vondel, Spee, Shakespeare, Donne, Sponde, and more, that in death one dies to the earth by melting into a higher state of life.

Teresa rises as incense disappearing in fragrant clouds. The change is swift and marvellous, as instantaneous and unfathomable as original creation. After the first genesis in which God formed man out of the dust and breathed life into him, this is a form of future genesis in which Teresa, at the summons of God who gave her breath, gives it up to him 'in a resolving sigh.'

Six

The Mystical Bride

Now Teresa awakes to the fulfilment of the sky. The jubilant, poly-phonous conclusion (lines 121-182) is a vision of eternity beyond shapes, numbers, and time, beyond the limits of Pozzo's and Gaulli's vastest church ceilings, beyond laws of nature and describable experience. 'Ask not the tongues of men' is one aspect of the problem, 'Angels cannot tell' is quite another. The poetry is more metaphorical than ever, an imaginative reconstruction of many Christian heavens, yet an individual-ized form – 'a hundred thousand loves and graces, and many a mystic thing.'[118]

Myriads of angels swarm about, flying, flowing, seeming to cluster, then to pour off in streams. The atmosphere is heady. Everything is transilluminated by spirit, ethereally light in weight and colour alike. Gravity has no pull, motion no friction, bodies no conflict.

From this highest vantage point we realize that here, just as in the chapel, the higher levels in the Order of Grace transcend and yet embrace the lower, as in a Platonic scale. Though the essential design of earth-ecstasy-eternity is the same in both, Crashaw shows ecstasy flowing into eternity without any interruption of space or time, without any diminution in brilliance. Teresa of the earth is gathered up into Teresa in glory. In Bernini's version of her apotheosis there are (besides the saintly likeness of Teresa added later to the vault window) four wall-paintings showing scenes from her life – on the right, a scene of Teresa at prayer and an early vision of Christ piercing her with a nail, and on the left, a road scene with a figure on horseback, and another of Teresa kneeling before Christ[119] (PLATE XX). In the poem Teresa's eternity is a consummation on the highest level of all she has forsaken or mistaken below in her earthly life. Both are superb instances of baroque profusion and plenitude, Bernini's restricted only by limited space, and Crashaw's thanks to the medium, opening up a limitless sky of multitudes, motion bright fire, and intense light.[120] The abundance is amazing and the space, which goes on infinitely, seems to be simultaneously filled and freely moving. Sequence there is, yet in heaven everything seems to be happening at once. Among these multitudes Christ alone is a single entity, though Teresa and the Blessed Virgin as parts of Christ seem at moments also to stand away from the throngs. This panorama, too broad for ordinary vision is yet a picture of the Many in the One. As the *Vida* expresses it, 'I saw, for a brief time and without any distinctness of form, but with perfect clarity, how all things are seen in God and how within Himself He contains them all.' The pitch of the lines never falls, the pace never abates.

This final section has a design nevertheless. Underneath the elaborate art of many Spanish painters Roger Fry found an instinctive clearness of mind. What he is saying applies as well to Crashaw: 'Something of the significance of pure form lurks behind all the complexity and extravagances of their devotional art.'[121] This design is the culminating phase of the marriage narrative. The triple movement of Teresa's arrival, the transfiguration of her former life, and the preparation for the Mystical Marriage, is really one movement.

In this supersynesthetic realm things masquerade as people, abstracts and concretes exchange places, fluids solidify, solids dissolve, parts stand for wholes. Already forecast earlier in the poem with such oddities as Teresa daring to drink a cup of cold deaths, or angel-souls finding smiles for their faces, eccentric statements now roll out in abundance. Kisses heap up, 'works' clothe the saint, hearts strike fire, vows beget virgin-births, flames kiss the divine light, and according to Crashaw's eloquence of love, the Virgin, as 'revealed life' *teaches heaven* to Teresa's *lips* with her *hand*. But above all, earthly things rise transformed into angels who join other angels in the marriage retinue. Once having existed as her 'good works,' 'rare works' (of writings), vows, woes, pains, sorrows, sufferings, tears, wrongs, deaths, and wounds, all these come into sudden being as angels. Similarly, the dart, wound, flame, and heart reappear from below now illuminated with maximum brilliance. And the Virgin, as the white mistress, the mother, the moon, the teacher, and the smiles of heaven, is imagined not only to glance on Teresa beatifically but to '*dart* her mild rays through thy *melting heart*.'

The apotheosis is Teresa of the past turning into Teresa of the future, her works of reform etherealized like the 'rare works' she wrote to record 'Love's noble history.' With the softer sounds of divinity are mingled the broken beats and rough edges of a language recollecting the earth.

> All thy old woes shall now smile on thee,
> And thy pains sit bright upon thee,
> All thy sorrows here shall shine,
> And thy sufferings be divine.
> Tears shall take comfort and turn gems,
> And wrongs repent to diadems.
> Ev'n thy deaths shall live, and new
> Dress the soul that erst they slew.

'Ev'n thy deaths shall live': the mood of timelessness signifies an end of time and an end of death when Teresa's purpose of proving 'how much less strong is death than love' reaches fruition.

Coming 'home' to her 'old friends' and the 'sons' of her vows (her converts seen now as the offspring of Christ and Teresa in the Mystical Marriage), she prepares for the bridal ceremony. At this point her brilliance sounds strikingly like St Teresa of the *Vida* in one of her visions: 'I thought I saw myself being clothed in a garment of great whiteness and brightness.' Attended by angels, dressed in a flaming robe of thousands of souls, she comes forth and bows to her 'sov'reign spouse.' Teresa of the *Vida* rises like a phoenix out of the fire of death to 'walk in the way of the Lord.' Yet Teresa the bride is not one bride in one ceremony but part of the brilliant collective soul which everlastingly goes to 'walk with him those ways of light.'

Fire and flame endure the intense change of ecstasy and dissolve into light. As the divine fire of Love consumes her, something different is visible in heaven. Once a child who breathed 'all fire,' then a martyr burned by the divine flame of ecstasy, in heaven this fire is transformed into cool brilliance. All at once it has no heat. All at once her bliss is cool and moonlike, and her tears turn to gems, in the presence of 'her snowy family.' This coming together of light, whiteness, coolness, and fruition is Crashaw's unique conception of heaven. The coolness recalls such single moments of celestial bliss as the historical saint felt during and after transports. 'When the rapture is deep, as I say, the hands become as cold as ice, and sometimes remain stretched out as though they were made of wood.'[122] In the ascent the soul having risen from the earth appears to pass through all the other elements. It is dark and dry in mortality, wet and hot in ecstasy, cool and light in eternity.

In heaven pain and effort disappear. Motion continues, rhythms persist, perhaps as metaphorical signs of the cosmic energy and harmony which affect the world below, but the freedom of heaven loses worldly tension and urgency. Doubt, error, and human limitation, the inescapable qualities of actual life described in the *Vida* and shown as symbols and human figures in the chapel, are all left far behind.

Intensity finally turns the poem into pure spirit, though the gently sensuous language never quite loses the memory and sounds of the earth. Resurrection of the body is still anticipated, and life in the body is still remembered. The same familiar sounds rise with the poem, the melodic line of one sound, the long *i*, seeming to tell the saint's story from beginning to end – *mild, kind, child, fire, die, sigh, life, thy, smiles, shine, eyes, bright, delight, white,* and *light.* The incantatory effect has been operating all along. That single sound, inflected up and down in its pendant position among other sounds, completes 'Love's noble history.' At the very close a spectrum of sounds, running from deep to high, seems deliberately to suspend the timeless, spaceless future by suspending the sound of long *i* for the last time.

> . . . who in death would live to see,
> Must learn in *life* to *die like* thee.[123]

It is a depthless sky. Scattered and intermittent beams of light constantly emanate from their single source in divinity, and return to it, to a singleness as broad as the universe. Time, which earlier deterred the soul's progress, is now limitless. And space, narrowed before on the road to martyrdom confined by ecstasy and the straits of death, opens out to infinity.

Part V

Epilogue

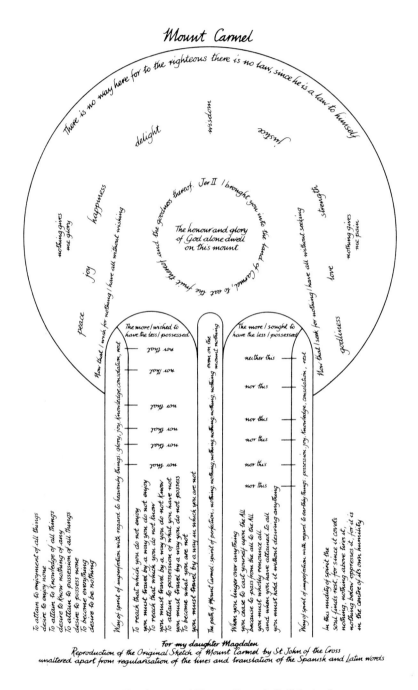

XXVIII The Ascent of Mount Carmel, St John's plan

Epilogue

'There is hardly any woman other than St Teresa who in total abandonment has herself lived out the situation of humanity.'[124] Teresa's ascent of Mount Carmel – down valleys of Aridity and over plateaus of Quiet to an invisible peak above the Sierra de Guadarrama – was fully as real as the literal, physical labours of founding new Carmelite houses. For Teresa, whom Machado describes as 'soul of fire' (*alma de fuego*), the broken Spanish terrain was a *mappa spiritus* two thousand miles from the original Carmel in northern Palestine.

Twenty-five centuries before Teresa's time Elijah, the last of Yahweh's great prophets and the legendary founder of the Carmelites, summoned the prophets of Baal in order to find out the true god by a test of fire (I Kings 18). It was agreed that he and the four hundred and fifty Baalite prophets would follow only that god who could consume the sacrificial offering with 'no fire under.' The Baalites called on their god from morn till noon. When he did not fire the sacrifice they cried aloud and cut themselves with their knives and lancets until the blood flowed, but all in vain. Then it was Elijah's turn. After summoning the people he repaired the broken altar of stones and dug a trench around it. He then piled upon it wood for the fire and upon the wood parts of a bull he had slain. After that he ordered water to be poured so plentifully over the altar that it drenched the sacrifice and filled the trench. 'Then the fire of the Lord fell, and consumed the burnt sacrifice, and the wood, and the stones, and the dust, and licked up the water that was in the trench.' Upon seeing this, all the people fell down on their faces and cried out, 'The Lord, he *is* the God.'

The ancient mountain of Carmel was a high and fertile extent of land spread out along the Mediterranean coast. Frequently regarded as an enchanted land, Carmel was said in the Old Testament to be 'favoured with the Divine Blessing,' and in the days of Darius the Great was thought to be sacred to Zeus, the father-god of the Greeks. Although the legendary history of the Carmelites dates from Elijah's time nine hundred years before Christ, the actual founding more likely occurred in the twelfth century A.D. when the Calabrian crusader Berthold settled on the mountain with ten other pilgrims. A few of the Carmelite brothers went to Europe soon after, and in the thirteenth century the Saracens drove the rest overseas to Tyre, Cyprus, Sicily, and beyond. Thus was the divine silence of Lebanon carried by the Carmelites to Europe. The same fire which kindled the faith of the Baalites was rekindled again and again in Spain, France, and England, in India, Persia, and the Americas, and once again kindled the faith of Teresa in the sixteenth century.

Still deeper in the past, in the myths which precede history and legend, there came into the world, perhaps at its creation, the primal fire of all fires. It may have been carried from dark caves, or across the water from the Orient, or from the workshop of Hephaestus somewhere in the upper air to make the forges in Etna and Vesuvius. There, in any case, the divine craftsman used it for his metal arts.

And from the beginning, fire was more than literal; more than an element, it was also a force, or a principle. From the timeless moment Prometheus stole it from heaven or from Hephaestus' forge, it existed for man's sake, as his power and his destruction. Prometheus carried it to earth in a fennel stalk so that man might realize his own creative nature. Forever ambiguously, man's arts and sciences would determine his future, to create or destroy, to give warmth and spirit to his total being, or to burn and annihilate it. At its worst, fire was the force that burned Empedocles in Etna, melted the wings of Icarus, streaked down as Zeus's thunderbolts to destroy his enemies, or, on the other hand, to kill Phaethon who came near burning up the world. But either way, fire was established as the central and most powerful of the elements. In the early Periclean age Heraclitus called the cosmos 'an ever-burning fire,' in Teresa's day Paracelsus said 'fire is life,' and in our own, Bachelard calls fire 'the active element at the centre of each thing.' As either element or principle, fire possessed the power to convert one thing into another, according to Heraclitus and the Milesian philosophers, and to produce the world in ever-repeated rhythms of life and death, so that always it 'again flashes up in fire, to arise from it anew, a phoenix.' Change is indeed the key to its nature.

Ever-changingly the same, free and fluid, formlessly formed, at the same moment moving and remaining still, fire is man's element, nearest us in our blood and birth, in our motives and our actions. The element most defiant of Nature's laws, it is essential to Nature's very existence. Yet fire is a becoming, a word or meaning which hovers between idea and actuality, man's subject and man's object, not always mastering man or mastered by him.

As the principle of creation and faith Greek soldiers, and then Roman, carried it alive in vessels. Its ambiguous nature followed, or led, the western tradition, and accordingly became the apocalyptic holocaust which will utterly destroy the world, but destroy it for the new life of the messianic kingdom. So its history is a broad record of purification by fear, sacrifice, and destruction – such as it was for Elijah. 'The seeds of Divine Fire' were for the Stoics the principle of growth which after the conflagration enable 'God' or Divine Fire to begin life again. And that has been fire's principle, in the vessels of soldiers, in the vestal temples of Rome, and, transformed to spirit, in the churches of Christendom.

We hear, in an uncanonical saying of Origen, 'whoever is near unto me is near unto the fire.' The Word, in some expressions, became Christ the firestone – the fire kindling new fires. As the rising, vertical element it unites earth with heaven. The fire of *Revelations* 'came down from God out of heaven, and devoured them.' But as the infernal fires of Dante burn, the purgatorial fires cleanse, and the paradisal fires shine. 'Is not my word like as a fire?' says the Lord, yet the same God comes to show man ascendence: 'For it came to pass, when the flame went up toward heaven from off the altar, that the angel of the Lord ascended in the flame of the altar.'

The Teresan experience is just this. She describes the fire of love as a 'great flame which seems to burn up and annihilate all life's desires.' The body is tempered by burning. The unity is unity of fire. Mystically mingled with water, the element which was at once most like and unlike it, fire loses the antipathy known in physical life. To Heraclitus as to Jung, polarity implies identity. The result is another unity. As Crashaw asks the Magdalene, 'Is she a flaming fountain, or a weeping fire?' One of those who had the answer was Tesauro: 'water and flame, once bitter rivals, are now reconciled in the Magdalene's eyes.'

There is in the epoch of Teresa, Bernini and Crashaw, the recurrent theme of fire as a unifying agent – in alchemy, in the archaic systems of Blaise de Viginère and Michael Maier, in Pascal's fervent cry to heaven: 'Fire, God of Abraham, God of Isaac, God of Jacob, not of the philosophers and scientists. God of Jesus Christ. Joy, joy, joy, joy of tears.' Very commonly the separation between human and divine, fire as element and fire as principle, disappears completely in divine transcendence – Jesus Christ is 'sweetest flame unmeasured' (Angelus Silesius), 'God is a spirit, a fire, an essence, and a light' (Friedrich von Spee), 'fire ascends, and I am all fire' (Jean Bertaut).

Crashaw, in his kind, writes a poetry of fire, not only in the Teresan poems but in about twenty elegies, hymns, and other poems. 'I die in love's delicious fire' are words from a 'Song,' and in 'The Flaming Heart Upon the Book and Picture of the seraphical Saint Teresa' he asks the heart to 'walk through all tongues, one triumphant flame.'

For Bernini's chosen subjects there was less occasion to use fire, either as metaphor or representation. It appears realistically in the early sculpture of St Lawrence on the grill. And if we credit the report of his son Domenico, while Bernini was working on the St Lawrence he thrust his leg into a fire in order to see the expression of a genuinely agonized face. In the later works when his manner becomes more symbolic, he spiritualizes fire. Bernini's St Teresa is a dream of ecstasy imagined into the eye, a flame-filled ecstasy, yet in their Teresan pieces both he and Crashaw move from substance toward essence, from the element of fire toward the spirit of fire.

In a treatise of 1626, Giarda explains that though visual images may appear as either symbols or direct representations, in the end the two are one. The purer a substance becomes the more it eludes the vision; fire fed by gross matter is made more visible to us. While the noblest arts are abstracts of the senses, their images 'can be grasped more easily, more clearly, and better' when they are substance and abstraction both. We therefore misunderstand an image, says a modern critic of Giarda, if we think of it only as a symbol of abstraction.[125] Like fire itself, an art must dwell with us in the intelligible world where, as it lives, it makes us aware of the supra-sensible truth.

> And it came to pass, as they still went on, and talked, that, behold, there appeared a chariot of fire, and horses of fire . . . and Elijah went up by a whirlwind into heaven.
>
> (I Kings 2).

Teresa also rises in the flame of Divine Love. Sometimes she distinguishes between fire (*fuego*), the primary, internal love of God, and flame (*llama*), the outward and upward radiations of love as it rises to its source in Divine Love.

> . . . the soul sometimes issues from itself, like a fire that is burning and has become wholly flame, and sometimes this fire increases with great force. This flame rises very high above the fire, but that does not make it a different thing: it is the same flame which is in the fire. . . . There is nothing more that I can say of it.

Except at the moment of mortal death, there is no real division between body and soul. Meanwhile life is the fire. It is the very Godhead, yet it is actual and earthly.

> The soul collects wood and does all it can by itself, but finds no way of kindling the fire of the love of God. It is only by His great mercy that smoke can be seen, which shows the fire is not altogether dead. Then the Lord comes back and kindles it, for the soul is driving itself crazy by blowing on the fire and rearranging the wood, yet all its efforts only put out the fire more and more. I believe the best thing is for the soul to be completely resigned to the fact that of itself it can do nothing.

Beyond Ávila, Rome, and Little Gidding, the Mystical Marriage is nevertheless consummated.

> . . . and all shall be well and
> All manner of things shall be well
> When the tongues of flame are in-folded
> Into the crowned knot of fire.

Notes

1 The main sources of Teresa's life are (*a*) her autobiography published posthumously as *Vida de Santa Teresa de Jesús* in the first edition of *Obras* (incomplete), ed. Luis de León (Salamanca, 1588); (*b*) the two earliest biographies: Fr. Francisco de Ribera, *Vida de Santa Teresa de Jesús* (Barcelona, 1809; orig. ed., Salamanca, 1590) and Fr. Diego de Yepes, *Vida de Santa Teresa de Jesús* (Buenos Aires, [1946]; orig. ed., [Madrid, 1599]); and (*c*) Alban Butler, *The Lives of the Fathers, Martyrs, and other Principal Saints* (12 vols., London, 1812-1815). Since the entry for St Teresa in *Acta Sanctorum* was published first in the mid-nineteenth century (the edition used here is: Rome and Paris, LV, 538-790), it depends on all the preceding works. Both early biographies are unusually good. Yepes (who was Philip II's Jesuit confessor and Prior of the Jeronomite convent in the Escorial) a priest well known for both his benevolent character and mellifluous style, was far less a scholar than Ribera (who was professor of Holy Scriptures at Salamanca). Ribera's work, begun long before Teresa's death, is based on what for that time was thorough and extensive investigation, and is remarkably (though not completely) free from prejudice, superstition, and the idolatry associated with sacred biographies. Further research, and correction of the *Acta Sanctorum* has been reported annually for eighty-five years in the *Analecta Bollandiana* (Brussels). The modern break-through in the study of St Teresa's life is recorded by Narciso Alonso Cortés, Américo Castro, Efrén de la Madre de Dios, Otger Steggink, and Antonio Domínguez Ortiz. Not all the work done by Otger Steggink and Crisógono de Jesús Sacramentado has yet been published (I am told by Professor Juan Bautista Avalle-Arce, University of North Carolina), nor has a new life by F. Marquez.

2 *Acta Sanctorum*, LV, 777-90, lists 63 Carmelite houses founded in Spain during St Teresa's lifetime. The total in Europe was at least 464 (over half in Spain; the rest primarily in Italy and France), although many were on other continents (e.g., 41 in Mexico). The *Catholic Encyclopedia*, III, 369, gives the grand total as about 590 in 1908, not including 100 Calced Carmelite houses.

3 This new knowledge comes mainly from: Narciso Alonso Cortés, 'Pleitos de los Cepedas,' *Boletín de la Real Academia Española*, XXV (1949), 86-110;

Américo Castro, *The Structure of Spanish History*, tr. Edmund King (Princeton, 1954), pp. 565-6; Santa Teresa de Jesús, *Obras Completas*, ed. Efrén de la Madre de Dios and Otger Steggink (Madrid, 1962), p. 4; Antonio Domíngez Ortiz, 'Historical Research on Spanish Conversos in the Last 15 Years,' in *Collected Studies in Honour of Américo Castro's Eightieth Birthday*, ed. M. P. Hornik (Oxford, 1965), p. 81. The birthplace was probably Majálbalago where her father and his brothers had lived. The grandfather was a *converso* of Toledo who was sentenced by the Inquisition for lapsing into Judaism. Her mother was from Valladolid. One episode which reveals Teresa's origin was a dispute between the Cepeda family and civil authorities over the family's refusal to pay municipal taxes, the family claiming they were *hidalgos*, not commoners, and therefore exempt from the taxes. That the Cepedas won their point with the civil authorities may be the source of the idea that Teresa was from the lower nobility. To judge from several of her letters to her brothers and the fact that all seven of them emigrated to Peru, it seems clear that Teresa herself knew of her Jewish blood.

4   Castro, *Structure*, pp. 84, 566.

5   J. P. de Oliveira Martins, *A History of Iberian Civilization*, tr. Aubrey F. G. Bell (London, 1930; orig. ed., Lisbon, 1879), p. 248. For Spain's leadership, and particularly the role played by Charles V, see Hubert Jedin, *Geschichte des Konzils von Trient* [up to 1597] (2 vols., Freiburg, 1949 and 1957), I, 179-94, 413-19; II, 181-95, 359-70.

6   Butler, XII, 57-9. This excludes the twenty-six martyrs of Japan, the martyrs of China, and the nineteen priests hanged at Bril by Calvinists. There were at least sixteen Spanish saints from the period 1550 to 1650, eleven from the Spanish peninsula: Paschal Baylon, Ignatius Loyola, Thomas of Villanova, Lewis Bertrand, Francis Borgia, Teresa of Ávila, Peter of Alcántara, John of the Cross, Francis Xavier, Francis Solano, and Joseph Calasanctius; and five others from Spanish territories: Andrew Avellino, Turibius Leon, Camillus de Lellis, Rose of Lima, and Joseph of Cupertino. Even though the figures may not be exact and the places associated with a saint not always unambiguously Spanish, it is certain that the largest number of saints in that era were Spanish, with Italian and French saints next in order. Butler's total list of about 1300 saints by 1650 brings out that the largest number of canonized saints lived between the third and seventh centuries, especially in the fourth and seventh.

7   Mysticism does not appear at random in religious history, according to Gershom G. Scholem in his highly illuminating and authoritative introduction to the subject of mysticism as a whole, in *Major Trends in Jewish Mysticism* (3rd ed. rev., New York, 1954), pp. 6-9. Rather, mysticism expresses a certain stage of spiritual consciousness, the third and final stage in the growth of a religion, whether it be Christian, Jewish, or Islamic. The argument runs as follows: at

first the scene of Man's relation to God is the scene of Nature. Consciousness is unified and the attitude is mythical and pantheistic (as in the modern world) until an awareness of the abyss between Man and God develops. Religion in fact destroys 'the dream-harmony of Man, Universe, and God' by making clear the difference between finite Man and infinite, transcendental Being. 'Man becomes aware of a fundamental duality, of a vast gulf which can be crossed by nothing but the *voice*,' the voice of Man in prayer and of God directing Man and propounding the laws of His revelation. In this second, classical stage the scene of religion is no longer Nature but the moral and religious action of Man alone and in community. Here religion is more completely separated from the mystical than at any other point. Though the abyss between Man and God can of course never be bridged, the effort continues. Once this point in religious history is reached, once the communal way of living and believing has been achieved, the phenomenon of mysticism can occur. This is the romantic stage of a religion, and it depends on the desire to cross the abyss between God and Man which one knows to exist. The mystic then undertakes a quest for the secret that will close the gap. He seeks 'to bring back the old unity which [formal] religion has destroyed, but on a new plane, where the world of mythology and that of revelation meet in the soul of man.' Thus the soul becomes the scene of action and the soul's journey through the multiplicity of things in the abyss to the experience of Divine Reality becomes its main preoccupation. In his pursuit the mystic seems to transcend formal religion and revive mythical thought, but without becoming the spiritual anarchist he is generally made out to be. The mystic (and Teresa is an instance) does not lose his allegiance to his religion. In the end mysticism emerges when these new impulses are somewhat contained within the form of the old religion rather than breaking through the shell of the old system to create a new one. The substance of scripture and tenets of a faith 'is melted down and given another form as it passes through the fiery stream of mystical consciousness.'

8 Twenty are represented in E. Allison Peers' *Studies of the Spanish Mystics* (2 vols., London, 1927 and 1930) and *The Mystics of Spain* (London, 1951).

9 Peers, *Studies*, II, 42, 57, 63-4, 66, 74, 125-6, 136, 151-7, 160, 166-7, 174-7, 187, 254, 289-90, 351-2, 376, 384-5, indicates the other writers she knew or who knew her by eulogizing, anthologizing, or imitating: Bernardino de Laredo, Juan de Ávila, Jerónimo Gracián, Cristóbal de Fonseca, Tomás de Jesús, and Juan Falconi.

10 Gerald Brenan, *The Literature of the Spanish People* (Cambridge, 1951), p. 166.

11 For a simple, fully informed account, see Anthony Blunt, *Artistic Theory in Italy 1450-1600* (Oxford, 1940), chap. VIII (even though this does not reach the period of Bernini and Crashaw).

12 E. Allison Peers, *Mother of Carmel* (London and New York, 1945), p. 18, says the first could have occurred in 1539. But in *The Complete Works of Saint Teresa of Jesus*, tr. and ed. E. Allison Peers (3 vols., London and New York, 1946), I, 319-20 (*Spiritual Relation*, IV) Teresa herself suggests that her visions began about 1555 and in her autobiography (*Works*, I, 155) from 1559 or so. It may be noted that in 1726 Benedict XIII made the vision of the Transverberation a feast in the Carmelite calendar.

13 No thorough investigation of the iconography of St Teresa, and examination of the paintings (and other works) has been made for this study. However, the major written sources are these: Fr. Gabriel de Jesús, *La Santa de la Raza: Vida Grafica de Santa Teresa de Jesús* (4 vols., Madrid, 1929-1935); Louis Réau, *Iconographie de l'Art Chrétien* (3 vols., Paris, 1955), III, 1258-62; A. Pigler, *Barockthemen* (2 vols., Budapest, 1956), I, 463-4; Cécile Emond, 'L'Iconographie Carmélitaine dan les Anciens Pays-Bas Méridionaux' (Brussels, 1961), XII, fasc. 5 of Collection in 8°, Deuxième série. Mémoires, Classe des Beaux Arts, Académie Royale Belgique; Enrique Pardo Canalís, 'Iconografía Teresiana,' in *Goya*, 53 (1963), 298-307; and the photographs and records of the Warburg Library, London, and the Frick Collection, New York. Of other sources, Émile Mâle, *L'Art Religieux . . . Après Le Concile de Trente* (2nd ed., Paris, 1951; orig. ed., Paris, 1932), pp. 161-7, is not very dependable; Margaretta Salinger, 'Representations of Saint Teresa,' *Metropolitan Museum Bulletin*, VIII, no. 3 (1949), 97-108, adds nothing new of importance; and Hye Hoys, *L'Espagne Thérésienne* (Brussels?, 1892?), I have been unable to find. For reference purposes, it may be useful to set down the names (excluding those marked 'att. to') of the other painters, print-makers, and sculptors mentioned in these sources: Alonso del Arco, J. B. Barbé, Giovanni da Bologna, (?) Besnard, Th. Boyermans, Alonso Cano, (?) Carracci, Antonio Cerveto, St Nicolas-de-Chardonnet, Gianbettino Cignaroli, Claudio Coello, Adrian Collard and Corneille Galle, Richard Collin, Jean-Baptiste Corneille, (?) Crespi, Walthère Damery, Jean Daret, Gaspard de Crayer, Gerard de Lairesse, Benedetto Gennari, Jr., J. B. Herregouts, Victor-Honorius Janssens, Jean Jouvenet, Nicolas Lauwers, Nicolas Loir, (?) Mancini, Pablo Mateis (or Matheis), G. Mentessi, (?) Messager, (?) Palomino, Pietro Paolo Raggi, Sebastiano Ricci, Alcázar Tejedor, Andrea Vaccaro, Norbert Van Reysschoot, (?) Viladomat, Anton Wiericx, Johann Andreas Wolf, and Peter Ykens. Anonymous versions of Teresa are in the Prado ('La Comunión de Santa Teresa'); Couvent des Carmes Déchaussés at Gand ('Le Maître de la Religion'); Couvent des Maricoles at Bruges ('Glorification de sainte Thérèse, Saint Ignace, Saint François-Xavier, Saint Philippe de Néri'); Eglise de Carmes Chaussés at Lille; church at Harmignies ('Sainte Thérèse Ecrivain et Docteur'); church at Lissewege.

14 Castro, *Structure*, pp. 84, 342, 346.

15 For a fairly useful general account of Teresa's writing, see Rodolphe Hoornaert, *Saint Teresa in Her Writings*, tr. Joseph Leonard (London, 1931; orig. ed., Paris, 1925), pp. 227-49.

16 The few details not in Teresa's writing come from Marcelle Auclair, *Teresa of Ávila*, tr. Kathleen Pond (New York, 1959; orig. ed., Paris, 1950), pp. 26, 468, and John Beevers, *St Teresa of Ávila* (New York, 1961), pp. 8-9.

17 The best source I know is in *Works*, III, 190-1 *(Book of Foundations)*.

18 Peers, *Studies*, I, 222, and A. Morel-Fatio, 'Les lectures de sainte Thérèse', *Bulletin Hispanique*, X (1908), 17-67, consolidate the evidence.

19 This is the opinion of one of her foremost modern critics, Crisógono de Jesús Sacramentado, in *Santa Teresa de Jesús* (Barcelona, 1936), p. 126.

20 This is reported not in the *Vida* but in *Works*, I, 352 *(Spiritual Relation*, XXXV).

21 A good account of the Convent of the Incarnation is in Hoornaert, *Teresa*, p. 38.

22 See note 2.

23 The equivalents I have borrowed from Father E. W. Trueman Dicken, *The Crucible of Love* (London and New York, 1963), pp. 396-403; after the unvarying *unión, visión*, and *estasis* (or *extasis*), come *arrobamiento* (trance), *arrebatamiento* (rapture), and *impetu*.

24 For proverbs, see A. A. Parker's fine piece, 'The Humour of Spanish Proverbs,' *Diamante* XIII (London, 1963).

25 Father Dicken's book on St Teresa and St John of the Cross is the most learned and illuminating study in English. My account of the contributions these two made to the study of mysticism has been informed by much in this book (chief references: pp. 173, 205-6, 395, 420-1). David Knowles's most recent book is *What is Mysticism?* (London, 1967).

26 *Works*, II, 79-80.

27 In particular, Gabriel de Jesús, *La Santa*, III, 224, and Auclair, *Teresa*, pp. 105-6.

28 *Works*, I, 192-3. She mistakenly wrote 'cherubim' for 'seraphim.'

29 *Works*, I, 145.

30 That the reception was enthusiastic I take from Italo Faldi, *La Scultura Barocca in Italia* (Milano, 1958), p. 37. No evidence is given.

31 The tract, referred to by Rudolf Wittkower, *Gian Lorenzo Bernini, The Sculptor of Roman Baroque* (2nd ed., London and New York, 1966), p. 254, is published by Giovanni Previtali, in 'Il Costantino messo alla berlina o bernina su la porta di S. Pietro,' *Paragone*, XIII (1962), 55-8.

32 According to James J. Gibson, *Perception of the Visual World* (Boston, 1950), p. 65, note 6, what a painter actually reproduces is 'the microstructure of the light reflected from these surfaces.'

33 For a superb exposition of this area of illusionism, see E. H. Gombrich, *Art and Illusion* (London and New York, 1960), especially pp. 211-22.

34 Filippo Baldinucci, *The Life of Bernini*, tr. Catherine Enggass (London, 1966; orig. ed., Florence, 1682), p. 77.

35 In George Kubler and Martin Soria, *Art and Architecture in Spain and Portugal* (Pelican History of Art, London, 1959), p. 237, Professor Soria refers to the midway position of 'realism' as a way to overcome the difficulty of spiritualism and naturalism being in apparent conflict while at the same time recognizing the bond between them.

36 Baldinucci, *Bernini*, pp. 83-5.

37 Sieur le Chantelou, *Journal de Voyage du Bernin en France* (Paris, 1930; orig. ed., Paris, 1885), p. 88. Baldinucci, *Bernini*, p. 78, gives an interesting instance of Bernini using a kind of *alla prima* technique in order to achieve spontaneity and lifelikeness in doing the bust of Louis XIV:

> In order to make the portrait of His Majesty the King of France Bernini first made many models. He removed all these models when he set to work in the presence of the King. When the monarch, wondering at his actions, asked why he did not want to make use of his work, Bernini replied that he had used models in order to introduce into his mind the features that he had to trace, but that once they had been envisaged and it was time to make them manifest, such models were no longer necessary: on the contrary, they impeded his purpose which was to conceive a likeness of reality rather than a likeness of the models.

37[a] Professor Wittkower has referred me to the account given by Valentino Martinelli in *Commentari* X (1959), 204-27 (Novità Berniniane 3. Le Sculture per gli Altieri').

38 John Pope-Hennessy, *Italian High Renaissance and Baroque Sculpture* (3 vols., London, 1963), Text vol., p. 121, says Bernini's early portrait bust of Paul V makes the break with the Roman portrait and has 'a sense of movement that no bust carved in Rome had ever had before.'

39 Baldinucci, *Bernini*, p. 75.

40 This account of Bernini's *concetto* I take from Rudolf Wittkower in *Art and Architecture in Italy 1600 to 1750* (Pelican History of Art, 2nd ed. rev., London, 1965), pp. 108-10, and in *De Artibus Opuscula XL. Essays in Honour of Erwin Panofsky*, ed. M. Meiss (New York, 1961), pp. 502-5. Pope-Hennessy, Text vol., p. 108, makes the same point about the early mythological subjects: behind them is Bernini's intention 'to provide a visual embodiment of a literary text.'

41 Baldinucci, *Bernini*, p. 74.

42 Wittkower, Bernini's most learned and revealing expositor, in *Bernini*, p. 30, describes the chapel as the ascending realms of Man, Saint, and Godhead. I have

interpreted the pavement as the level of mortal death below the other three in order to keep the emphasis on ecstasy in its relation to life, death, and after-life.

43 The latter observation is Nikolaus Pevsner's in *An Outline of European Architecture* (Penguin Books, 7th ed., Harmondsworth, Middlesex, 1963), p. 255 (the actual wording is: 'the most daring example of such illusionism in Rome').

44 This is a cryptic version of Wittkower's fine account in *Bernini*, pp. 17-24.

45 How definite the plan was is not clearly known. Irving Lavin sounds uncertain about it in *Art Bulletin*, 38 (1956), 256, and so does Wittkower, *Bernini*, pp. 18, 20.

46 Baldinucci, *Bernini*, p. 35.

47 Irving Lavin tells me that we know no date for the commission. The first record we have, found by Mr Lavin, is for January 1647, before which no work could have been done on the chapel. (An inscription with the date 1647, which was once in the pavement, alludes to the time of the chapel's founding, not, as is usually said, to the time its architecture was completed.)

48 Bernini's showing Teresa without sandals may be a literalism (*descalzo*) which suits the simplicity of treatment (treatment of costume, that is). And his showing the angel at her right side, rather than her left, may allow the angel to hold the dart more naturally in his right hand.

49 A good reason for selecting the left transept, on the outside wall (the last chapel to be occupied was the one opposite, in 1694) was Bernini's plan to build this house on the outside of the building.

50 See Herbert Read's discussion in *The Art of Sculpture* (London and New York, 1956), pp. 46-9.

51 Read, *Sculpture*, p. 71: 'The specifically plastic sensibility is, I believe, more complex than the specifically visual sensibility. It involves three factors: a sensation of the tactile quality of surfaces; a sensation of volume as denoted by plane surfaces; and a synesthetic realization of the mass and ponderability of the object.' See also 'La Sensibilité Plastique de Sainte Thérèse de Jésus' in Michel Florisoone, *Esthétique et Mystique* (Paris, 1956).

52 The drawing is no. 11 in *Disegni del Bernini*, ed. Luigi Grassi (Bergamo, 1944).

53 The identifications are taken from Wittkower, *Bernini*, p. 217. Sometimes it is erroneously said that the figure of the Doge is Bernini himself. Pope-Hennessy, *Sculpture*, Catalogue vol., p. 131, thinks Baldinucci's reference to 'the last Cardinal Cornaro' must mean that Cardinal Federigo is the figure reading in the left group, but positive identification was made by Lucia Casanova, 'Un illustre personaggio veneziano in S. Maria della Vittoria a Roma,' *Bollettino dei Musei Civici Veneziani*, 1958, 2, 13-14, and underscored by Wittkower's observation of the care given to the figure (for instance, the deeply incised eye surfaces of this figure alone).

54 Pope-Hennessy, *Sculpture*, Catalogue vol., p. 131, says something baffling about this: 'the relevance of these figures is not to the group behind the altar but to the altar itself.' My position is that they are relevant to both.

55 Wittkower, *Italy*, p. 103.

56 A much neglected aspect of baroque churches is the marbles. Thanks to the generous assistance of John P. Ward Perkins, Director of the British School at Rome, prof. Raniero Gnoli of the University of Rome, and dott. Cesare d'Onofrio of the Biblioteca dell'Istituto di Archeologia e Storia dell'Arte, some tentative identifications of marbles in the Cornaro Chapel can be made. This will serve only until Mr Lavin's book on the chapel gives us an authoritative account of them. Some idea of their individual patterns and their arrangement in the chapel can be gathered by looking at the Plates, beginning with those nearest the central statue and going down the two sides of the chapel to the pavement and altar rail. First, primarily those seen in Plates XXIII, XVIII, and IX. The large panel behind the statue is alabaster. The pilasters (and corner pieces right and left rear, and front corners) are *verde antico* from Thessaly. The columns are *africano* from Teos. The panels below the columns are onyx, possibly *onice turco* (Turkish onyx) and those below the sculpture, Egyptian onyx. The large side panels and the panels below them are also onyx, and the frames around the side panels and the boxes at the sides are *giallo antico* from Numidia (more exactly, *marmor numidium* from Shentou). The strip running across just below the statue and bases of the columns is *breccia di sette bassi* from Skyros (the scrolls flanking the altar front are made of the same). The very narrow strip below the other is *bianco e nero antico*, a rare marble probably from the Pyrenees. The strip going across below that strip, and below the panels, is *breccia traccagnino* or *arlecchino* (perhaps Greek). Plate XV shows, on the side walls, door frames of *rosso* from France (not ancient). Down toward the pavement (Plate IX) the broad strip at the level of the altar face is *africano* and the wide grey panels running across at the bottom are probably *bardiglia* from Carrara. The skeletons are also *giallo antico*, surrounded by *nero* (from Belgium?), and encircled with inlay of *giallo antico*, *rosso*, and *nero*. Other panels there are *breccia corallina*, *broccatello di Spagna* (brocaded), and *porta santa* from Chios. The altar is of *diaspro tenero* (Sicilian jasper), and the rail and balusters (see Plate VIII again) are Calabrian *bianco nero* and poor quality *giallo antico*.

57 Emilio Lavagnino et al., *Altari Barocchi in Roma* (Rome, 1959), p. 24, may have something like this in mind: 'la graduazione delle luci e del colori dei marmi . . . ,' but movement and unity are the points of emphasis here.

58 Wittkower, *Italy*, p. 217.

59 Read, *Sculpture*, pp. 105-23, is plain and valuable on this subject.

60 Again, even learned and careful critics persist in seeing parts of the work in isolation: Antonio Muñoz in *Roma Barocca* (Rome, 1928), pp. 324-5, says the

seraph has 'un sorriso malizioso,' even though malice or mischief (or in this case any kind of humour) seems to have no relevance whatever.

61 This observation is based on looking at most of the well-known churches of *seicento* Rome, and is substantiated by the opinion of Professor Irving Lavin. In addition to decorative marbles, glassed-in images of the dead also occur quite commonly, but almost nothing else. This aspect of altars seems not to have been studied, and little assistance is given where one might expect it, in the section 'Dekorative Ausstattung des Stipes' in Joseph Braun's *Der Christliche Altar* (2 vols., Hamburg and Munich, 1924). Emilio Lavagnino *et al.* (see note 57) is also silent on the subject. Incidentally, in that same volume Luigi Salerno remarks, p. 84, that the Cornaro Chapel relief of the Last Supper is derived from one in S. Giovanni in Laterano ('. . . non è del Bernini, ma una copia che un certo Alpini eseguì di quello analogo di Orazio Censore in S. Giovanni in Laterano, sostituito anch'esso con una copia in età napoleonica').

62 William James, *Varieties of Religious Experience* (New York, 1929), pp. 347-8.

63 Simone de Beauvoir, *The Second Sex*, tr. H. M. Parshley (New York and London, 1953; orig. ed., Paris, 1949), p. 673.

64 *Vida*, chap. 40.

65 Lione Pascoli, *Vite de' Pittori, Scultori ed Architetti Moderni* (2 vols., Rome, 1730 and 1736), I, 207 (in 'Gio. Batista Gaulli').

66 Henri Focillon, *The Life of Forms in Art*, tr. C. B. Hogan (2nd ed. rev., New York, 1948; orig. ed., Paris, 1934), p. 6.

67 Read, *Sculpture*, pp. 88-91.

68 Baldinucci, *Bernini*, pp. 7, 72.

69 This palm tree receives the attention of Giulio Carlo Argan, on the cover and at p. 126 of *The Europe of the Capitals 1600-1700*, tr. Anthony Rhodes (Geneva, 1964).

70 Baldinucci, *Bernini*, p. 74.

71 It is the thesis of Herbert Read's *The Art of Sculpture* that, until Rodin, sculpture does not fully exploit the sculptural qualities of marble. At the same time, with the partial exceptions of Read and Wittkower, one is impressed by how little is said about the sculptural qualities of Bernini's work by most of his critics, including Pope-Hennessy, Gombrich, Italo Faldi, Muñoz, and Pevsner.

72 Stendhal (Marie Henri Beyle), *Œuvres Complètes*, ed. Paul Arbelet (30 vols. and 3 supp. vols., Paris, 1913-1940), II, 104 ('Promenades dans Rome').

73 Even as sensitive and masterful an interpreter as John Pope-Hennessy, *Sculpture*, Text vol., p. 110, urges that Bernini was 'free of the least trace of introspection,' even though he simultaneously speaks impressively of Bernini's artistic intelligence (e.g., Text vol., p. 124, 'The expression of the sitter may be evanescent,

and the action in which he is presented may be transitory, but neither was an arbitrary choice, and each bust presupposes a close knowledge not of the features only but of the mind behind the mask'). How can you have close knowledge of 'the mind behind' without being introspective? A good deal of critical opinion has the same intellectually superior tone and makes the same error of confusing learning and introspection. However much Bernini knew, in the bookish sense, we need only look at the work itself to find an unusually introspective artist.

74 Adrian Stokes expresses the idea almost this way in *The Quattro Cento* (London, 1932), pp. 130-1.

75 James Lees-Milne, *Baroque in Italy* (London, 1959), p.132, mistakenly says the painting was by Bernini, while in fact Heinrich Brauer-Rudolf Wittkower, *Die Zeichnungen des Gianlorenzo Bernini* (2 vols., Berlin, 1931), I, 166-7, makes clear that Bernini only made a drawing for this 'Sangue di Cristo' which Spierre then engraved, and which Gaulli then probably executed as a painting, after the engraving. Brauer-Wittkower, II, 198, reproduces the engraving, and also, in II, 128, Bernini's original as well. An illuminating discussion of the subject occurs in Francis Haskell's *Patrons and Painters* (London, 1963), p. 82.

76 Baldinucci, *Bernini*, pp. 72-3, is translated in approximately these words.

77 Variations among the editions of this poem are seldom important. Yet the 1648 version in the second edition of *Steps to the Temple* is clearly the best, since it is the last one Crashaw saw and it improves on the 1646 edition of *Steps to the Temple* in almost every instance of change, and since the posthumous version of 1652 in *Carmen Deo Nostro* shows itself to be careless and lacking in understanding in seven noteworthy instances (including the omission of lines 61 and 147). As the poem is printed here, only two verbal departures are made from the 1648 version (at lines 47 and 72), but punctuation, spelling, contractions, and capitalization have all been modernized, with only those capitals retained which are names for Jesus Christ (and not all the names, since 'spouse' is left as the texts have it, and so are 'he' and 'him'). The most serious departures are in punctuation, which affects meaning and also shows how fluid and how tightly coherent the poem is. At lines 9, 162, and 172 dashes (they might have been colons) have been added to assist comprehension. The punctuation is very sticky in lines 165-75, at two points. I follow the 1648 version again in making a sentence break at 'Go now' (line 169). Lines 171-5 Crashaw appears not to have smoothed out perfectly; I make a new sentence start there, for sense, and make 'My rosy love,' which is bracketed in the texts, into the object of 'put on' (also Christ's words), and treat the remainder as appositional to 'love.' The paragraphing follows the 1648 version. As it appears here, the subtitle of the hymn comes from the editions of 1646 and 1648, and the main title from that of 1652, which reads in full: 'A Hymn to the Name and Honor of the Admirable Sainte Teresa, Foundresse of

the Reformation of the Discalced Carmelites, both Men & Women; a Woman for Angelicall Heigth [*sic*] of Speculation, for Masculine Courage of Performance, more then a Woman. Who yet a child, out ran maturity, and durst plot a Martyrdome.'

For an authoritative, comprehensive account of the texts, see *Poems*, ed. L. C. Martin (2nd ed., Oxford, 1957), pp. xliii-liv.

78 The best account of Bernini's theatrical activities is Irving Lavin's review of Bernini, *Fontana di Trevi*, ed. Cesare d'Onofrio (Rome, 1963) in *The Art Bulletin*, 46 (1964), 568-72. Other details may be gathered from Baldinucci, *Bernini*, pp. 83-4 and Richard Bernheimer, 'Theatrum Mundi' in *The Art Bulletin*, 38 (1956), 242-3, as well as from Chantelou, Evelyn's *Diary* (17 November 1644), and the *Enciclopedia dello Spettacolo* ('Bernini'). The trick of the spectators seeing themselves was accomplished by actors placed in a second theatre opposite the first who wore masks which very accurately resembled the features of the real spectators. That only began a whole evening of tricky diversion (for which the tickets of admission were made of very costly majolica).

Irving Lavin's highly illuminating review saves me from a conventional, well-published error: that Bernini was the *inventor* of stage machinery (e.g., fires and floods) which was his main contribution to the baroque theatre. As far as is known, he invented none of them. Moreover, the important thing to him was 'to have ideas' and to let others work up the scenery and stage machinery. His 'secret' lay in 'the *way* he used the techniques of [stage] illusion.' He went one step beyond what was usual by manipulating the stage tricks in ways which involved the audience as participants, as 'actors,' in a production. This included deliberately making the tricks fail and staging fake accidents (e.g. the torch which 'accidentally' threatens to burn down the theatre). The plot of Bernini's only published play (generally, but incorrectly, referred to as *Fontana di Trevi*) shows the chief figure, a master of stage effects, failing to make them work right. Thus he served the intentions of amazing and delighting an audience. An interesting sidelight on Bernini's illusionism in general is the variation he makes on the play-within-a-play. As Lavin says of the misnamed *Fontana di Trevi*, 'it is not strictly a play that contains a play, but a play about the creation of a play.' Characters of the inner play partly duplicate characters of the main plot, 'the chief character of the main play actually holding a conversation with his fictitious self.'

79 These items are in Wittkower, *Bernini*, pp. 268-9 and 276-7 (Table). Those things he designed or decorated for Queen Christina are described in Georgina Masson, *Queen Christina* (New York, 1968), pp. 249-51, 253.

80 Baldinucci, *Bernini*, p. 79, and Domenico Bernini, *Vita del Cavalier Gio. Bernino* (Rome, 1713), p. 29.

81 The point is made by Helen C. White, *English Devotional Literature 1600-1640* (Madison, Wisconsin, 1931), pp. 222-3.

82 George Williamson, in *Six Metaphysical Poets* (New York, 1967), p. 124, thinks it probable that Joseph Beaumont wrote the unsigned preface. He gives no evidence.

83 *The Poems, English, Latin, and Greek of Richard Crashaw*, ed. L. C. Martin (2nd ed., Oxford, 1957), p. xlviii, where Martin casts doubt on the suggestion of 'Thomas Car' (Miles Pinkney in actuality) that Crashaw did all twelve of the engravings in this volume, if in fact that is what Car really is suggesting (see *Poems*, p. 235). Mario Praz, *Studies in Seventeenth-Century Imagery* (2 vols., London, 1939), I, 205, points out that most have other initials, and thinks that Crashaw may have done no more than two. Incidentally, the title *Carmen* may be a pun or double pun: besides being a play on Thomas Car as the subject of the opening poem (which introduces the anagram HE WAS CAR), *Carmen* may also be an echo of Teresa's Carmel. Such puns and conceits were a commonplace of the age, whether verbal or visual (cf. Bernini's Neptune garment). The Dutch painter Judith Leyster used the sign Ï (pole-star); Mme de Rambouillet called herself Arténice (an anagram of her given name, Caterine); John Bunyan converted his name into the phrase NU HONY IN A B (IOHN BUNYAN); etc.

84 Lorus and Margery Milne, *The Senses of Animals and Men* (New York, 1962), pp. 3-11, 137, 149, 157-73, 189-90, 211, 275-7. Beyond the 'five senses,' different degrees of scientific recognition have been given to the senses of weight, pressure, motion, proximity (sensing near objects in the dark), direction, and some internal senses like thirst and hunger. Many overlap or combine with others, many substitute for other, as in synesthesia.

85 This is essentially what Northrop Frye says in 'Music in Poetry,' *University of Toronto Quarterly*, 11 (1941), 175-6. Crashaw is not to be grouped with poets often unwarrantedly called musical, such as Chaucer, Pope, Tennyson, Keats, and Swinburne, but with those who carry over into poetry the sounds, the rhythms, and sometimes the forms of music, such as Skelton, Smart, Browning, Hopkins, and Auden.

86 In this connection see the interesting piece by Gladys R. Reichard, Roman Jakobsen, and Elizabeth Werth, 'Language and Synesthesia,' *Word*, 5 (1949), 224-33.

87 The process was so deliberate that George Chapman devotes the five parts of *Ovid's Banquet of Sense* (1595) to each of the five senses, and Marino symbolizes the five senses in five gardens he creates in *Adone* (1623), and Phillip von Zesen treats the effects love has on the five senses, in *Adriatische Rosemund* (1645).

88 Focillon, *Form*, p. 13.

89 *Idem*, p. 13.

90 René Wellek, *Concepts of Criticism* (New Haven and London, 1963), p. 111.

Wellek's whole essay in this volume ('The Concept of Baroque in Literary Scholarship,' pp. 69-127) strikes me as the most helpful and judicious account of the concept that I know.

91 The best perspective on this is Frank J. Warnke's in *European Metaphysical Poetry* (New Haven and London, 1961), pp. 1-86, which can be extended toward the Baroque with Lowry Nelson, Jr.'s valuable introduction to *Baroque Lyric Poetry* (New Haven and London, 1961), pp. 3-17. One other title may be added: Odette de Mourgues, *Metaphysical, Baroque, and Précieux Poetry* (Oxford, 1954), pp. 1-6, to show how theory of terminology serves only to bring one back to the poetry.

92 T. S. Eliot, *Selected Essays* (New York, 1932), p. 246, and frequently elsewhere.

93 For Crashaw's reputation, see Joseph E. Duncan, *The Revival of Metaphysical Poetry* (Minneapolis, 1959), pp. 30, 35, and index. For the Coleridge reference, see *Coleridge's Miscellaneous Criticism*, ed. T. M. Raysor (Cambridge, Mass., 1936), p. 278.

94 Quoted from *The Religious Poems of Richard Crashaw*, ed. R. A. E. Shepherd (London, 1914), p. 9.

95 Carol Maddison, *Apollo and the Nine* (Baltimore, Maryland, 1960), pp. 360-1, has recently made this point.

96 Austin Warren, 'The Mysticism of Richard Crashaw' in *Church Quarterly Review*, 116 (1933), 85, makes a case for Crashaw's having read Juan de los Ángeles, Luis de León, and Diego de Estella, as well as St John of the Cross. But this book on Crashaw, *Richard Crashaw, A Study in Baroque Sensibility* (Ann Arbor, Michigan, 1957; orig. ed., Baton Rouge, Louisiana, 1939) omits the point.

97 The two are by W[illiam] M[alone], Antwerp, 1611, and by M. T. (almost certainly Tobie Matthew), Antwerp, 1642. A third, said to be 1623 and perhaps the first edition of Tobie Matthew's translation, has not been identified by the main bibliographical authorities (BM, BN, Palau, Gillow, Halkett-Laing, Hazlitt, Lowndes, Otilio del Niño de Jesús, Pollard-Redgrave).

98 This is line 11 of 'An Apology.'

99 *Times Literary Supplement*, 2 July 1964, p. 578: Allan Pritchard, 'Puritan Charges Against Crashaw and Beaumont.'

100 Warren, *Crashaw*, p. 52, surmises that Crashaw's conversion occurred in 1645 shortly before he left England. Perhaps. We know only that he had become a Roman Catholic by September 1646 when Henrietta Maria wrote to the Pope on his behalf (letter printed in *Poems*, ed. Martin, p. xxxiii).

101 This is Warren's opinion, *Crashaw*, p. 51.

102 To Warren's account should be added a record found by P. G. Stanwood, *Notes and Queries*, 211 (July 1966), p. 256. Several times (first on 28 November

1646) Crashaw's name appears in the Pilgrim Book, a register of visitors to the English College at Rome.

103 These references are to line 155 of 'A Hymn,' line 28 of 'The Flaming Heart,' and lines 2-3 of 'An Apology,' but there are others too: line 82 of 'A Hymn' – she 'writes thy spouse's radiant name / Upon the roof of heav'n'; line 20 of 'An Apology' – 'thine own dear books'; and line 20 of 'The Flaming Heart' – 'her pen.'

104 The names of Christ (or Love in Christ) spread right across the poem, at lines 2, 9, 50, 56, 74, 82, 143, 154, 178.

105 Ribera, *Teresa*, p. 96; Yepes, *Teresa*, pp. 21-2.

106 Simone Weil, *Waiting on God* (tr. Emma Craufurd, London, 1951; orig. ed., Paris, 1950), p. 108.

107 Mario Praz, *The Flaming Heart* (New York, 1958), p. 247.

108 Roger Fry, *A Sampler of Castile* (Richmond, Surrey, 1923), pp. 7-8.

109 This really occurs as four divisible phases which flow as one: 79-96 (first dart stroke), 97-104 (cry of bliss), 105-9 (Teresa's reaction), and 110-17 (exhalation to heaven). Even in the first phase Divine Fire becomes her fire: God's dart, dipped in the 'rich flame' of her heart, is her pen writing God's name on the roof of heaven.

110 Jacques Maritain, *Creative Intuition* (New York, 1953), p. 3.

111 The two quotations are from Ernest Mundt, *Art, Form, and Civilization* (Berkeley, 1952), p. 116.

112 The distinction is frequently drawn, e.g. by Charles Williams, *Descent of the Dove* (London, 1939), pp. 57-62; by Mario Praz, *Imagery*, I, 12-13; and by Warren, *Crashaw*, p. 147 (who has Augustine, Eckhart, and St John of the Cross on the philosophical side, and Suso, Catherine of Siena, and Teresa on the imagistic side).

113 Jean Seznec, *The Survival of the Pagan Gods*, tr. Barbara F. Sessions (New York, 1961; orig. ed., London, 1940), pp. 103, 105; and Praz, *Imagery*, I, 142, 159.

114 Praz, *Imagery*, I, 139, 142.

115 Rosemary Freeman, *English Emblem Books* (London, 1948), p. 164.

116 This according to Freeman, *Emblem*, p. 166, and *The Works of George Herbert*, ed. F. E. Hutchinson (Oxford, 1941), p. 567.

117 Richard Norton, *Bernini and Other Studies* (New York, 1914), p. 32, thinks the seraph's nose and smile resemble a Greek *panisk* (minor deity attendant on Pan, 'little Pan') more than a heavenly messenger.

118 *Poems*, ed. Martin, p. 129.

119 These identifications, here indicated only sketchily, come from complex and diverse sources of biography. Fortunately they are to be made entirely clear by Mr Irving Lavin in his forthcoming book on the chapel.

120 In Crashaw's hymn, the words for brilliance are *diadems, crowns, stars, gems, snowy, sparkle*, and more often, *shine, white, light*, and *bright* (six times).

121 Fry, *Castile*, p. 8.

122 *Works*, I, 289.

123 *Thee*, though it refers primarily to Teresa, may well refer to both her and Christ at once.

124 Simone de Beauvoir, *Second Sex*, p. 714.

125 E. H. Gombrich's 'Icones Symbolicae' in *Journal of the Warburg and Courtauld Institutes*, 11 (1948), 163-92, is an introduction to Giarda's work, including a commentary which is highly relevant to this discussion.

Index

Superior numbers refer to notes

ROBERT T. PETERSSON

Robert T. Petersson is Professor of English at Smith College, where he teaches Renaissance and seventeenth-century literature, classical literature, and late Renaissance painting and sculpture. He is the author of *Sir Kenelm Digby: The Ornament of England* (1956), and is the editor of Shakespeare's *King Richard II* in the Yale Shakespeare series. He earlier taught at the University of Chicago and Yale University and received his doctorate from Princeton University.